MW00961204

A Year Without

THE GROCERY STORE

KAREN MORRIS

To Steve, my wonderful husband: without you none of this would have been possible. I depend on you. I am so thankful for you and your support through this process. The Lord knew exactly what he was doing when he gave me to you.

Table of Contents

ACKNOWLEDGMENTS

To my kids, Ian, Jordan, Shannen, Ethan, and Nathan. Thank you for your snuggles, hugs, kisses, patience, and support during the process of writing this book.

Ally, you are such a huge part of this book. You kept me on track when it was easy to bail. You reminded me that missing a self-imposed deadline wasn't the end of the world. I can't wait to see your book finished and published. It will be amazing!

Niki, thank you for your craziness! It's exactly what I need when I get tunnel vision.

To my launch crew: Valerie Jones, Joanne Jones, Johanna Repke, Whitney Creath, Heather Malone, Angie Cornell, Melissa Edens, Jessica Crosmun, Noreen Dreste, Heather Estey, Miquilaue Young, Marcie Eubanks, Raquel Evans, Clarinda Olenslager, Amenda Friedl, Ryder Church, Blythe Edwards, Audrey Burke, Jennifer Moore, Steve Melton, Jennifer Hill, Sheri Duff, Jill Gevjan, Jull Kirby, Catie O'Mathers, Jill Underwood, Gayle DosAnjos, Tracy Lynn, Torbjorn Karisen, Coral Emerson, Theresa Gerdes. Thank you all so much for making this dream a reality. You're the best!

Chapter One
What You'll Find in My Basement

A year without the grocery store … really? Is that a thing? And even if it is a "thing," why would I want to do it? *Could* I do it? Do I *need* to do it? *HOW* do I do it? Where would I keep all the food?!

Maybe the thought of not having to set foot in a grocery store for a year seems like more of a fantasy than a tangible possibility. Maybe even the thought of planning three hundred and sixty-five meals makes you freeze in your tracks.

But what if I told you that you don't have to come up with three hundred and sixty-five *different* meals to eat? What if I told you that in a ten-foot by sixteen-foot part of my basement, I have a year's worth of food—and a month's worth of water? Now, what if I told you that it didn't cost me as much as a year's worth of food costs most people? If I wanted to, right now, I wouldn't have to set foot in a grocery store for an entire year.

It's not a fantasy for my family; it's a matter of reality.

But why?

What would possess me to go out and purchase extra food for my family? I don't believe the world as I know it will end tomorrow or next week. I don't have a super-secret bunker into which my family and I will disappear for ten years and then re-emerge hoping to find the world a better place. I'm just a mom of five children (ages fifteen, fifteen, eleven, eleven, and six). I make sure my kids get up, get ready for their day, and do their schoolwork. I run them to their various activities. We attend church. If you met me on the street, you'd never know what was in my basement—nor would I tell just any "Joe" what I stash down there, but I will tell you.

Are you ready for my super-secret formula to what I keep down there?

I keep peace and confidence down in my basement. I keep a sense of security stashed next to my barrel of "I can rest well tonight." I keep the smiles of my children on the same shelf as my hubby's sighs of relief.

All of those things are a result of my year's worth of food storage. I have planned and stored a year's worth of food, so I can sleep well at night because of my sense of peace. I have confidence in our situation no matter what may happen at my husband's job. I know my children will smile because they will be well fed even during a power outage or an ice storm, and my husband will sigh with relief knowing that he still has coffee even if we wake up without electricity.

Other things I keep hidden away in my basement are extra free time, significant money savings, variety in my family's diet, a calm evening (even with unexpected company), and the light in my kids' eyes when they find out they are having their favorite meal for dinner.

My food storage saves me significant money over my family's regular grocery menu. I don't have to spend time each week incessantly planning new menus or shopping for hours on end, giving me extra free time. Unexpected company is no problem at all. I can always double (or, if need be, triple) any recipe that I'm making. I keep plenty of my children's or husband's favorite meals on hand because I know it will make them smile.

That's a pretty tall order for a ten-foot by sixteen-foot space in my basement.

Yes, it is true, according to the Bureau of Justice Statistics, that 83 percent of current twelve-year-olds will experience a violent crime sometime in their lives[1]. It's much more likely that that same twelve-year-old talked about in the article is going to experience a power outage—maybe even in the middle of the winter. They will be without electricity at some point in their life—probably within the next year. At some time in their life they're going to experience inclement weather that will affect their plans by trapping them in. Maybe they live in a hurricane-prone area or tornado alley. Maybe someday they or their spouse might get laid off from a job, or work hours or pay could be drastically cut. What if a wage-earner gets hurt on the job and can't work for six months or more?

Well, that depends. I know that our family would have a food cushion if any of those things ever happened to us. What about you?

Let's talk about something a little more common. What happens if there's a snowstorm? You can't get out because the roads are thick with ice or snow. The power has gone out. How are you going to cook? How are you going to prepare the food that you have in the house? How much food

---

[1] https://www.bjs.gov/content/pub/pdf/llv.pdf

do you have in the house? When you hear there's going to be a snowstorm, do you run through the stores, grabbing the last loaves of bread and gallons of milk? Wouldn't it be a lot safer for you to already have food in your house so you can prepare healthy and delicious meals without having to leave? Knowing that you can even prepare them without power is a bonus so that you don't have to be one of the ones out there scrambling to get bread, milk, candles, and rock salt.

If there's a power outage in the summer, depending on where you live, it can get very, very hot. How do you cook your food and not heat your house further? Which food should you use? You don't want to open your fridge because you'll let out a lot of the cold air.

Besides being sensible and important, one of the best reasons to work on building your food storage is that, depending on how you go about it, food storage can actually save you money compared to regular groceries. For example, if I buy a canister of oatmeal at Aldi, I pay $0.20/cup of oats. If I buy the same type of oats in bulk through a co-op called Azure Standard, I pay $0.11/cup of oats.

That's almost half the price!

Learning to follow sales and only stock up on what's on sale saves a lot of money. Add learning how to use coupons effectively on top of those sales and you save even more. There are economical ways to stock your pantry for a fraction of what you would normally pay.

Food storage is about being proactive and taking steps to keep my family safe because *something could* happen. "Be Prepared" is more than just the Boy Scouts' motto.

And anyone could do it—everyone *should* do it! You don't have to be a Mormon or a Doomsday prepper.

Practice Makes Perfect

The last thing we need to hit in this first chapter is that we need to practice. This is one of the fundamentals of food storage preparation. There is such a simple reason for this. One time, I had decided on a menu that included scrambled eggs, and realized that I was out. My daughter reminded me that we had some powdered eggs, so I used the recipe on the side of the can that described how much egg powder and how much water to use to reconstitute the eggs.

I whipped it up and put it in a pan thinking, "I'm going to scramble these up just like regular scrambled eggs, and they are going to look and taste just like scrambled eggs." Well you know what? We ended up tossing them because they didn't look or taste like scrambled eggs in any fashion except for the color.

When you practice using your food storage, you find out what will and won't work. You need to find out that you have the wrong ingredients before you're snowed in. Maybe you thought your recipe called for tomato powder, but it called for diced tomatoes. You also need to make sure that your recipes taste good. You want figure out if you need to use certain spices to make your meal more palatable, or if you cook it a certain way, it works better. You need to learn all these things and practice ahead of time.

Another reason to practice is that oftentimes when you are cooking from food storage, you need to turn your meal out quickly. Perhaps you have a family who is waiting on this meal because either the power has gone out and they've been working hard to set things in order or because good food helps assuage fright. Suddenly, you've got to make a meal, and you've got to make it from scratch from your food storage.

If you are learning on the fly, it is so much harder to do and you're going to feel real pressure. There's a good chance that it's not going to turn out well the first time. I know that I've tried a couple of new recipes lately, and not necessarily food storage recipes. You think, "Okay, I know how to cook, and I've been cooking for a lotta years, so this should work." Then it turns out tasting bad or it's the wrong consistency, or it crumbles. You learn that it's not going to work. So you think, "Maybe if I tweak it this way, and I try it again." After a couple of weeks, suddenly, the kids are saying, "Hey Mom, this is really good. I really like this," when they didn't anticipate that they were going to like it in the first place.

Practicing with your ingredients is important, but you also need to practice with your methods. The first time we pulled out our solar oven, we made up some scones. According to the oven's instructions, at our latitude we should be able to cook in all four seasons in our solar oven. It was a bit nippy outside, but, hey, we had it pointed at the sun. We had it tilted the right direction. Two hours later, they still were not baking, and there was a little bit of condensation on the inside. It really wasn't functioning. I was so glad that I tried it before I needed to use it to cook. No one wants to depend upon something that they really haven't tried before.

Maybe you've seen someone cook something before, and you think, "Hey, I could do that!" but you've never tried it yourself. That's a recipe for disaster.

I've seen people cook with a Dutch oven. It is a totally amazing process. A Dutch oven is a large cast iron pot with three legs. The person cooking pulled some coals from a fire and sat the Dutch oven right on top of the coals. They poured the ingredients for cornbread into the Dutch oven, put the lid on the pot. Then they scooped some coals out of the fire and set them on the lid of the cast iron pot. After five to ten minutes, the lady lifted the lid and looked down in to the pot to see how the cornbread was doing. She decided that it needed to go longer, but that the bottom was probably baking faster than the top was, so she moved the pot, swept the coals back into the fire, and returned the pot to its previous place. All of that takes time to learn. We need to realize, "Okay, I need to check it now. Okay, it looks like it's cooking too much on the bottom, so this is what I do." Honestly even just lifting the lid without spilling any of the coals into the cornbread was amazing, but all of those things take practice.

Something else that you're going to find out with practice is if you have broken equipment. You might think, "I have this pressure canner. If something happens, and we are without money and can't go to the grocery store, I will learn how to pressure can." Maybe you've never used your pressure canner before. What happens if the pressure canner is broken? You're going to be up a creek without a paddle, but if you are practicing with your equipment beforehand, that's something you'll find out while you can still do something about it.

To recap, there are definite reasons why everyone should have some kind of food storage. It doesn't mean you have to have a year or even six moths, but you need something deeper than your average pantry. There is a philosophy of food storage that will make a difference in this world, and then practicing how you do your food storage is going to be so crucial to your success.

In the next chapter, we're going to get into the nitty gritty of food storage: what is it, how does it work, and how to afford it.

Chapter Two
Long-Term Food Storage The Theory

If you were to descend into my basement right now, you'd find a fairly normal-looking room. While there are block walls, they are painted. There is carpet on the floor. We have a desk, a table, a twin bed, a bunk bed, and two rocking chairs. If you were my guest for a night and decided to venture past that into what we call our laundry room, you'd find a washer and dryer, but that's not what would draw your attention. No, your eye would be drawn by eight large shelving units and a workbench filled with food storage items—both food stuffs and equipment. If you were even a little more curious, and you turned the opposite direction and ventured around our hot water heater, you'd find about 50 five-gallon buckets lined with Mylar bags and filled with different items from rice to dried milk powder to beans and wheat.

But it wasn't always that the case.

Everyone must start somewhere. This chapter is all about where to start. When I think about food storage, I think of it as a savings account. If something happens, a savings account covers your deficit in funds. If something happens and you can't purchase food, your food storage is your food savings account. According to CNBC.com, 78 percent of Americans are currently living paycheck to paycheck[2]. That means many people reading this book are living paycheck to paycheck. How would you feel if you knew that you didn't need to go grocery shopping for three months? What about the radical idea of not having to shop for a whole six months or even for a whole year? Would that take a weight off your shoulders and allow you to relax just a little? Food storage can help you accomplish just that.

In this chapter, we're going to be discussing everything that goes into food storage. We'll talk about terms like short-term food storage, long-term food storage, #10 cans, and buckets. We're going to discuss the basics of getting started with food storage. How do you figure out what kind of

---

[2] https://www.cnbc.com/2017/08/24/most-americans-live-paycheck-to-paycheck.html

things you should store? Should you just go buy cans of lots of different things? How can you build your food storage affordably? In a pinch, how can you provide your family with a year's worth of food storage for $160 per person? I'll tell you how.

What is Food Storage?

What is food storage? At the risk of sounding simplistic, it's food that's stored to eat at a later date.

There are two distinct types of food storage: short-term food storage and long-term food storage. I liken short-term food storage to a very deep pantry. You have someone coming over for dinner, and you couldn't go grocery shopping last week. You go to your pantry and find something that you already have all the ingredients for that you can whip up quickly. Food storage is going to completely take care of the situation. Or if you have children, there's that ever-present question of "Hey mom. What's for dinner?" That can be answered by your short-term food storage. In practical terms, short-term food storage means always being ready for a series of meals without needing to go to the grocery store. Short-term food storage's purpose is to get you through small crises or to get you over the hump in a long-term crisis.

Long-term food storage is made up of basic ingredients, which can be stored for twenty years or more. These are also generally foods that you cannot reasonably grow or cultivate yourself. Oftentimes, long-term food storage is comprised of #10 cans and four- to six-gallon buckets. A #10 size can holds just under one gallon of food. Picture those large metal coffee cans you see in the grocery store—that's about the size of a #10 can. In terms of types of food, long-term food storage is usually comprised of items such as rice, oatmeal, wheat berries, dried beans, spaghetti, macaroni, non-fat powdered milk, flour, sugar, brown sugar, honey, molasses, maple syrup, baking powder, baking soda, and more.

When deciding between short-term and long-term food storage, you may be surprised that it's better to start with long-term food storage first. Long-term food storage can be put together in much less time, with much less money, and take care of your family for longer than short-term food storage. There are three main types of long-term food storage: variety buckets, prepackaged ingredient buckets, and buying in bulk and packaging the ingredients yourself.

Variety Buckets

These are buckets containing a variety of different meals, usually sealed in Mylar to keep oxygen, water, and light out of the containers. A variety bucket might contain several servings of oatmeal, of chicken à la king, of chili, tortilla soup, powdered milk, and orange drink. The meals themselves may be different, but that gives you an idea of what could be found inside.

A variety bucket means that you are going to get a variety of different foods. You're not going to eat the same thing every day; instead, you'll have different meals. Each meal will be sealed for you in Mylar. Each meal is as simple as add water and eat. These buckets are *easy* to use.

That ease, however, comes with a price. These buckets are very expensive. At the time of writing this book, Costco currently sells a Deluxe Survivor Variety Food Storage Buckets for about $190 + tax. They break the contents down for you: it will feed one person 1,916 calories a day for six weeks, two people 1,916 calories a day for three weeks, or four people 2,012 calories a day for ten days.

If you are a single person, that might be just the way to go. Pick up eight of those and you'll have food for an entire year for around $1,600. The problem is when you get into families. Using that bucket, a family of four would need three of those per month. After tax they may end up paying $600 for one month of food or $7,200 for a year's worth of food. The more people you have in your family, the more cost prohibitive they can be.

Prepackaged Ingredient Buckets

The second type of long-term food storage is prepackaged ingredient buckets. A prepackaged ingredient bucket is a five- to six-gallon bucket prepackaged with one ingredient and generally sealed in Mylar with oxygen absorbers. Think of a six-gallon bucket of flour, a six-gallon bucket of salt, a six-gallon bucket of sugar, a six-gallon bucket of macaroni. Those are types of prepackaged ingredient buckets.

These have some great advantages to them. You can choose things that your family will eat. One of the main rules of food storage is that you only buy food that you know your family likes. There's no point in purchasing a long-term bucket if you aren't going to appreciate eating each food in it. Another advantage is that these buckets are cheaper than a variety bucket. When you buy a five-gallon bucket of flour, it's going to be a whole lot cheaper for you than if you buy a variety bucket, because you can make thirty different meals with it. You might be surprised at what you can make with flour. Check out Chapter Nine for some great ways you may not have thought about using flour.

Emergency Essentials has around twenty different five-gallon buckets with different ingredients. They call these SuperPails. These include things like beans, wheat, sugar, cold cereals, oats, rice, powdered milk, popcorn, and other items At the time of this writing, for five-gallon buckets of cereal are approximately thirty-five dollars, while beans are eighty dollars, and wheat is fifty dollars. You can do so much with wheat, sugar, rice, milk, oats, and beans. The prices are better than the variety buckets, but there is a much more economical way to store your food long-term.

Buying in Bulk and Packaging the Ingredients Yourself

Buying in bulk and packaging the ingredients yourself is by far the cheapest way to purchase long term food storage, you just have to package it yourself. There are only a few things to buy: the ingredients, the buckets, the Mylar bags, and oxygen absorbers. For example, if I purchase wheat berries from a company called Azure Standard, it would cost me about twenty-seven dollars (after shipping) to fill a five- or six-gallon bucket. The Mylar bag and oxygen absorber would cost me another two or three dollars. I could package my wheat berries for around thirty dollars for a six-gallon bucket. This is a savings of twenty dollars over a bucket prepackaged for me. If you have a Latter-day Saints cannery near you (you don't have to be a Latter-day Saints member to use their cannery), the cost would be even less.

Where to Purchase Foods for Long-Term Storage

So what types of foods should go into long-term food storage? Some examples are oats, wheat berries, dried beans, legumes, powdered milk, sugar, flour, pasta, potato flakes, freeze-dried apple slices, corn, and corn meal, honey, salt, baking soda, coffee (very important), bullion products, and raw alcohols like whiskey or vodka. All of those work very well for long-term food storage.

The biggest question that most people ask is from where do I get these things? There are four main types of places to get these things: bulk foods stores, co-ops, online food storage companies, and local LDS canneries.

Bulk Food Stores

For your bulk foods stores, you can find long-term food storage items at Costco, Sam's, and BJ's wholesale. You should be able to find things like #25 bags of flour, #10 bags of sugar, #25 bags of rice, containers of coconut oil, bulk spices, and even some freeze dried foods from time to time.

There are so many benefits to using bulk food stores. Most of the time, you get a big bang for your buck. I find new items that can contribute to my food storage efforts all the time at my bulk food store. One of the newer items that caught my eye was freeze-dried hash browns in six family-size serving containers packaged together. These contribute enormously to my food storage efforts. I also find good sales on meat. I may not be able to freeze-dry my own meat, but I can pressure-can the meat for later use, saving my family a lot of money over the course of a year.

One of the other things that I appreciate about the bulk food stores is that I can pick up items which aren't necessarily food items, but can help immensely in my food storage. My local Costco carries vacuum sealers with jar attachments. These help if I'm trying to store my herbs long-term or if I'm making up meals in a jar for future use. I have found my favorite knives at my local bulk foods store. High-quality blenders help as I'm preparing many of my foods for storage. The list could go on and on.

Bulk food stores have their downsides too, however. You do have a yearly fee to shop at most of them. This needs to be taken into account when considering the savings by buying in bulk. You also have to be careful—while you will find many good deals there, there are many items that cost more per unit than their standard grocery store equivalents. You have to be on the lookout for the good deals and make sure you don't get pulled into buying a larger package. Don't immediately think that it's a better buy than you'll find at your regular supermarket.

Online Co-ops

The vast majority of my long-term food storage comes from a co-op called Azure Standard. Azure sells many things, in anywhere from small quantities up to large, bulk quantities. The larger the quantity you order, the less you pay per pound. Azure is where I get my oats, cornmeal, salt, baking soda, beans and legumes, pasta, rice, honey, and so many other things. I can buy a five-pound package of non-aluminum baking soda for around five dollars. I can get 25-pound packages of bean soup mix for around thirty-five dollars. I purchase all my bulk spices through Azure at a fraction of the cost I could get them at the store.

Azure Standard is a co-op. You go online and sign up—absolutely for free. There is no monthly commitment or items to order. You sign up for a local "drop," and each month they have trucks that go out across the US. The company tells you the day and time of your drop. Either you or a friend needs to be at the drop point at the time they tell you, and you pick up your order then.

Bulk Foods Section at a Regular Grocery Store

Sometimes your regular grocery store will have a bulk food section. Whole Foods and HyVee have bulk foods section. If you offer to buy items by unit (which may be a #50 bag or a #25 bag depending on the item), oftentimes they will give you a discount. I know Whole Foods historically has given a 10 percent discount when you purchase items in bulk.

Unless you are purchasing specialty items because of dietary issues, the bulk foods section of most regular grocery stores is still going to be more than you would pay at your local bulk foods store or through a co-op like Azure Standard. If, however, you have someone in your family who is gluten free and you have to purchase certified gluten-free oats, then the bulk foods section of your local grocery store may be the way to go. Do make sure you check prices against online stores to see if the grocery store is the most cost-effective option.

Online Food Storage Companies

Because food storage has gone mainstream, food storage companies have cropped up which cater to people who are seeking to provide their families with properly packaged food that will last. Some of these companies include Thrive Life, Emergency Essentials, Augason Farms, and eFoods Direct. Food storage companies mostly specialize in short-term food storage, but you can sometimes purchase seventy-two-hour buckets, which are designed to feed a family of four for 72 hours in case of a power outage, month-long variety buckets, a year supply of food, or five- or six-gallon single ingredient buckets. Emergency Essentials has long-term food storage buckets at some of the best prices per bucket. They can be found at www.beprepared.com.

Latter-day Saints Canneries

The last place that I would recommend for finding your long-term food storage is a local Latter-day Saints cannery. I am not Mormon. My mom, however, worked with a person that was a Mormon, so Mom put me in touch with her.. I started going to the LDS cannery outside of St. Louis, Missouri with my mom's co-worker. I purchased a variety of items here— wheat berries, flour, potato flakes, rice, macaroni, sugar—all for very low prices. One of the remarkable things about working with an LDS cannery is that you can either purchase the bags or you can stay and together with others, you split bulk ingredients into #10 cans (think coffee-can-size), put an oxygen absorber into the can and seal the can with a specialized machine. Then you leave with whatever #10 cans that you ordered when you arrived. Since they are packaged this way, they are much easier to transport than five-gallon buckets. You don't have to worry about the ingredients going bad since a smaller container is used up more quickly.

The Most Efficient, Cheapest Way to Store One Year's Worth of Food

What if you haven't started any food storage? Because of the news or because we're going into winter, or tornado season, or hurricane season, you realize, "Yes, it really could happen to me." You decide that you want to jump in quickly and feel like your family would be able to eat no matter what happens.

If you need to provide your family with one year's of meals in short order, there is a simple and relatively cheap way to go about it. Purchase or obtain four five-gallon buckets, four Mylar bags, four 2000cc oxygen absorbers, four twenty-five-pound bags of bean soup mix, two sixteen-ounce bottles of bouillon cubes, and 365 days of vitamins per person for your family. Bean soup mix is full of both protein and carbohydrates. Most bouillon cubes contain several different spices (almost all contain turmeric—an anti-inflammatory spice), which have different vitamins and minerals. The vitamins should cover most vitamin and mineral deficiencies for a diet like that.

For about $160 per person, you can feed your family for a *year*! If, like me, you have a large family then start by purchasing enough for one person. Do this every month until you have enough for your entire family, but if time is of the essence, purchase as much as you can and rest easy at night knowing your family will be fed.

The Importance of a Garden in Your Long-Term Food Storage Plan

Long-term food storage is great because it is comprised of things you normally can't grow or make yourself. But you won't get a diversity of nutrients with only long-term food storage buckets. What you're not getting in any of these buckets is fresh, live nutrition. You're not going to find five-gallon buckets with peas and spinach. You can get those freeze-dried (not in five-gallon buckets), but those are much more expensive.

Therefore, you need to have a garden for nutritional diversity. You need a garden for enzymes, for vitamins and minerals that you won't find in your buckets of long-term food storage.

Don't panic and think, "Well, that leaves me out. I can't have anything to do with long-term food storage because I live in an apartment," or "I rent a house and the owner won't let me put in a garden."

For the last three years, we have been renting. As a renter, we haven't been able to dig up our backyard to start a garden. It was time to get creative. Right now there are several tomato plants, strawberry plants, and some peppermint, oregano, basil, and spearmint in five-gallon buckets in the front yard. The garden is still very small. We're still learning, but we plan on moving to where we can plant a very large garden soon. This time without a conventional garden has given us a wonderful chance to learn about gardening.

Don't be concerned if you don't have acreage. You may be able to garden in a backyard. You can also rent a plot on which to garden. If we weren't able to get a new house here soon, our plan was to talk to a family that we know that has five acres and ask them if we can rent a quarter-acre plot so that we could garden on it. Other options include buckets on a balcony if you are living in an apartment. We have a family in our church right now that is looking to purchase vacant plots of land. Our city has some odd-shaped vacant plots that they are looking to off-load because they can't be built on because of their size or shape. Some of these are more than a quarter of an acre and these plots are being sold for $500–$600. You could buy a plot of land like that in the city, and you can garden.

The Type of Seeds You Use Is Important—Conventional and Heirloom Seeds

When we're talking about long-term food storage including a garden, we need to discuss seeds. There are two main types of seeds: conventional seeds and heirloom seeds. If you go to your local hardware store, Walmart, or Walgreens, you'll see inexpensive packages of conventional seeds. That package of seeds will be great for that year's garden, but you will have to buy those same seeds again for next year's garden.

Why not just save the seeds from plants like tomatoes or cucumbers and plant those the next year? If you are using conventional seeds, they have been grown in such a way that they will not produce a crop the following year. They want you *to need* to buy seeds from them every year.

Heirloom seeds are the second type of seed. These are seeds that have been saved for generations. If you plant an heirloom seed and get a productive tomato plant, you can take one or more of those tomatoes and if you save their seeds correctly, you can plant them the next year into more healthy tomato plants.

Make sure that you are looking at heirloom seeds from places like Seed Savers, Baker Creek Heirloom Seeds, and Victory Seeds. A book that I would recommend is called *Seed to Seed*. This book walks you through the process of how to grow food from seeds, harvest seeds from the food, and handle them properly so that they will successfully grow plants the following year. It discusses different ways to handle different types of plants, and different instructions on how to gather seeds from foods that you don't normally get seeds from like broccoli, lettuce, cauliflower, or asparagus.

Purchase more than one year's worth of seeds and put the extras away in order to have backups in case something happens that first year or two as you are learning to garden. In your first year gardening, if some seeds don't produce or the seeds are saved incorrectly, there will be a back-up set of seeds to use the next year.

Chapter Three will expand on the idea of long-term food storage. I'll share tips on how to get food storage buckets for as little as free. Even if you have to pay, I'll show you how to do it very inexpensively. I'll share my quality and inexpensive sources for Mylar bags and Oxygen absorbers. I'll talk about the enemies to proper food storage, and how exactly to go about packaging your own food, so you can save yourselves as much money as possible.

Chapter Two Assignments:

1. Determine a place for your garden.
2. Plan your garden and purchase seeds for foods your family will eat—even if you won't plant a garden until next year.
3. Answer the following questions: What long-term foods will I begin to store? How much of each food will I plan to store? When do I need to have these foods by?
4. Find the nearest canneries and contact them to find out current prices. Research the best prices you can find between local canneries, Azure Standard, and your local bulk foods store.

If you aren't sure where to find items mentioned in this chapter or you want my specific recommendations, you can find them listed in the Resource Center of the website:

https://www.ayearwithoutthegrocerystore.com/single-post/2017/12/07/Resource-Center

Chapter Three
Putting Long-Term Food Storage Into Practice

Packaging Long-Term Food Storage

During my first trip to the Latter-day Saints cannery, I picked up about five hundred pounds of food. It varied in type: oats, wheat berries, powdered milk, black beans, kidney beans, and probably several more things. If you had looked at my van as I drove out of the parking lot, the back would have been riding very low. I'm sure it looked rather comical.

When I got home, my husband helped me unload the bounty into our entryway where it sat tucked away under the stairs for at least a week. Looking at all those bags I thought, "I have to repackage all that?!" It both looked and felt very daunting. I was afraid I wasn't going to do something right, and I'd lose all that food when I repackaged it.

I decided Saturday was the day. My husband could keep the "chicklets" as I lovingly called our kids, and I would tackle that mountain. About forty-five minutes after I started, all the food was labeled and sealed in Mylar, in five- and six-gallon buckets ready to be taken to our storage room. I felt a huge weight lift off my shoulders. My mind had made it so much worse than it turned out to be, and we had a wonderful start on our food storage.

But it wasn't always that way for us. Even six years into our marriage, we were living off $1,200 a month as a family of four for over a year. We could have been one of the 17.6 million households—not people—who go hungry each year[3]. Even now for many of us, we could be just one life event away from joining those numbers, if we don't do anything about it now. So let's talk about what you can do right now to keep your family from becoming one of those statistics.

In this chapter, I'm going to walk you through the enemies of food storage and how to defeat them, how to obtain free or inexpensive supplies to repackage your food for storage, as well as how to repackage your food safely and properly, the "normal shelf life" of properly repackaged foods,

---

[3] https://www.rti.org/sites/default/files/resources/full_hunger_report_final_07-24-14.pdf

other affordable things that need to be added to your long-term food storage to make it much more palatable for your family, and how to practice cooking with your long-term food storage.

Enemies of Food Storage: Light

This is true whether you are storing food or water. You want to keep the light off of your food storage. Light causes food to deteriorate, and in water to grow bacteria and algae.

There are simple ways to take care of this issue. Many of these fixes will overlap between the different enemies of food storage.

Store your water in opaque, food-grade plastic. Most of the time, you'll see the containers colored blue. Blue does well at inhibiting light absorption and keeps algae production down. Make sure you are choosing food-grade blue containers.

Light can cause also food to break down. This is easily solved by putting your food into Mylar bags. While Mylar bags can easily be punctured, they can be stored inside plastic buckets. The Mylar inhibits light and the bucket protects the Mylar.

Oxygen

Have you heard of the term "oxidation"? When you hear it, I want you to think of a rusty nail. When the nail was manufactured it wasn't rusty, but with the presence of moisture and oxygen, the nail oxidizes or rusts. While food doesn't rust, it does oxidize in the presence of oxygen. Since the atmosphere on our planet is approximately 21 percent oxygen, it's a potential problem that we need to deal with when it comes to food.

The fix for this is so simple and easy. When you purchase Mylar bags to seal your food, you should also purchase oxygen absorbers. When used and placed properly, these handy little packets will save your food from oxidation.

These packets should not be confused with silica desiccant packets. You do not want to use both, as the silica removes any trace of moisture while the oxygen absorber requires a tiny amount of moisture (like the moisture in the air) to activate it.

Moisture

While oxygen absorbers require moisture to work, they don't require any more moisture than you would find in the air. Moisture is definitely an enemy of food storage. Moisture in long-term storage will begin to break down the food, causing the food to lose its integrity. It also can cause mold and mildew, and allow bacteria to grow which will destroy the food you have stored.

Food should be put into buckets at room temperature. What some people don't realize is that just because the food is "dry" when you put it in, that doesn't mean that it will stay dry if you don't keep the temperature steady.

Think of a glass of iced tea sitting on the counter on a warm summer day. What happens to the outside of the glass? Condensation forms on it because there is a temperature variation between the inside of the glass and the outside of the glass.

Another great example of this is single-paned windows. The house we are currently renting has single-paned windows. During the winter, the outside of the window is colder than the inside. This causes condensation on the inside of our windows. If that condensation isn't constantly and consistently cleaned up, mold grows on the inside of our windows.

If you put your food storage buckets in a place where they are subjected to temperature swings, the same thing that happened to my windows last winter will happen to the food inside your buckets. Condensation will form on the inside of the Mylar, allowing bacteria and fungus to grow and destroy your food. This leads me to the next enemy of food storage.

Temperature

You need to keep the temperature of your food storage consistent. As we saw above, food stored in Mylar can be destroyed by not keeping it in a consistent temperature. Other forms of food storage deteriorate much more quickly in hotter temperatures.

Temperature at which food is stored is important. The warmer the air temperature where you store your food, the shorter the time it will remain edible. Certain prepackaged food storage meals will keep for five years if you keep them at a steady fifty degrees. If you store those same prepackaged foods at sixty degrees, they are good for up to four years. If you stored them at eighty degrees, they are good up to three years, but if you stored them at 120 degrees like you'd find in an attic, they would only be good for one month.

The temperature at which you store your food storage will greatly affect the length of time that they will keep.

Pests

There are two ways that pests can destroy your food storage. They can destroy it by infesting it or by eating it. If food is stored improperly (not in Mylar and in buckets), pests such as rodents can easily smell the food. At one point in our food storage journey, we purchased three whole boxes of different food storage meals. We put some in our garage, stored in plastic totes surrounded by fabric. When we went to move and were going through our totes, we found that a rodent of some kind had gotten into our garage. It broke through the flimsy seal on the plastic tote and ate its way through the fabric to get to the food, which, of course, it ruined. We shouldn't have stored food in our garage anyway—we weren't taking into account the temperature swings and the high temperatures in the summer.

Pests can also eat your food from within. This might sound disgusting and make you want to purchase only prepackaged foods "just to be safe." Unfortunately, as scary as it sounds, prepackaged foods aren't always safe. Several years ago, we started to notice that we were seeing moths. First it was just a one, and then a couple of days later, we'd find another one. Soon though, we were noticing them with much more frequency. I went searching for the source of these moths.

We didn't have any unsealed food storage at that moment, but the only place (other than the kitchen) that we stored any food was in our storage room. When we discuss food storage organization in Chapter Six, you'll hear more about our food storage room. I perused the different shelving units in our storage room, and finally found worm-like larvae climbing toward the back of one of our shelves. I cleaned the larvae off and followed them back to the culprit. We had become infested with moths because a box or two of brownie mix that we purchased at the store were infested with moth larvae.

Time

There are two ways in which time is an enemy to your food storage. First, even properly packaged foods can lose nutritional value over time. Sometimes foods, like beans, won't necessarily lose nutritional value, but they can become hard to the point that they won't soften up, even if soaked. There are many foods that if repackaged properly will last up to thirty years, just don't expect the texture or taste to be exactly what it would have been if you packaged it yesterday.

If your food wasn't packaged or purchased with the intention of it lasting thirty years, you will need to keep expiration dates in mind. This oftentimes pertains more to short-term food storage than it does to long-term food storage, though.

Another way that time is an enemy to your food storage can be if you wait too long to repackage your foods. Another time when we went to the Latter-day Saints cannery and purchased about 200 pounds of wheat berries, I had the best of intentions of getting around to repackaging them "soon." With life as busy as it was at the time with four children, eight and under, I didn't get around to it soon enough.

Again, we started noticing a moth here and there. This time however, I wised up. I headed to our storage room and started looking for the culprit. I searched high and low to find out what had caused moths in our house. Unfortunately, this time, because I hadn't gotten around to repackaging our wheat berries in time, we lost all 200 pounds of it to moth larvae. That was quite a blow, not only to our food storage efforts, but to my ego, knowing it was my fault for not prioritizing the repackaging our food and losing so much of it to pests.

How to Properly Repackage Food for Long-Term Storage

Since we've talked about all the enemies to long-term food storage, we need to talk about how to keep those enemies at bay by properly repackaging the food you buy to store long-term.

1.) Always start by determining how much food you will be purchasing on any given run. This will help determine how many buckets and Mylar bags you are going to need.

2.) Obtaining your buckets is easy, but you'll want to get them for free! Free is easy, cheap is easier. The next time you go into a conventional grocery store with a bakery of any kind, head to the bakery and ask if they have any food grade buckets they are willing to give you. Normally, they purchase frosting in four- to six-gallon food-grade buckets. Most places will give these to you for *free* since they just normally throw them away. The most I've paid for food grade buckets from a grocery store is just a dollar per bucket. If you were to look up prices for buckets online, even through a company like Azure Standard, you'll pay at least six to eight dollars per bucket!

If you purchase your buckets used, once you get home, take the time to thoroughly wash them out with warm soapy and then rinse them down in a bleach solution to kill germs. Make sure to dry them thoroughly before using them. You need to start gathering buckets well ahead of time because most grocery stores throw out buckets each day, once they are empty. You may need to ask several places or go in on a few different days.

3.) Use the approximate amounts you determined above in #1 to help you determine how many buckets and Mylar bags you'll need. Fifty pounds of oats usually fills two and a half five-gallon buckets. Twenty-five pounds of wheat or beans will usually fill about one five-gallon bucket. Fifty pounds of sugar or salt will fill about one and a half buckets.

There are a few basic things about Mylar that are helpful to know. Mylar bags come in different sizes. Make sure you purchase the size that corresponds to your bucket size. Your oxygen absorbers should also be for the appropriate size container. If you are using a four- to six-gallon container, you can still use six-gallon Mylar bags and 2000cc oxygen absorbers. Make sure that you are purchasing the appropriate size oxygen absorbers. The first time I purchased them, I purchased 500cc oxygen absorbers because I didn't know any better.

Two places that you can purchase Mylar bags and oxygen absorbers are Azure Standard and MylarPro.com. I can get packages of twenty Mylar bags and twenty oxygen absorbers together as one item. Azure standard has the best deal, but if they don't have the right number of oxygen absorbers (you'll need to use all you buy in one packaging session), then MylarPro will be a better way to go.

4.) Once you obtain your food, put it into the freezer for one to three days to kill any insect larvae that may be in the bags. Then remove it from the freezer and let it set at room temperature for at least a day. This is important because you don't want to be putting cold food into room temperature bags because it creates moisture in the form of condensation, which will ruin your food.

5.) Start the packing process.

Gather everything in one place: Cleaned, disinfected, and dried buckets, room-temperature ingredients, Mylar bags, oxygen absorbers in their original package—do *not* open your oxygen absorber package yet!— a three-foot length of a two by four board, and a clothes iron.

Line up all your buckets.

Put a Mylar bag in each bucket. The bags will stick up above the top of the bucket. This is expected and totally fine.

Gather your ingredients.

Start pouring your ingredients into the Mylar bags. Make sure that your buckets are as full as they can be, but leave about four inches at the top of the bucket (not the bag) for the top of the bag once you seal it. Once you pour the ingredient into the bucket, pull up the Mylar bag, bounce the bucket up and down, then twist it left and right quickly. This allows the ingredient to settle into the bag so you can better determine how full your bucket is.

Put all your ingredients into all your buckets *first*. Don't do each ingredient from start to finish before you move onto the next one.

After you've filled each of the buckets that you're going to fill, get your two by four and plug in your iron. Let your iron get hot. Pull your Mylar bag up and straighten it as tall as you can. Then place your section of two by four across the mouth of your bucket. You're going fold the Mylar bag over the board and iron it as smoothly as you can, leaving a two-inch gap at the side. Do this for all your bags.

Once you've ironed all the Mylar bags two inches shy of being shut, you're going to open your oxygen absorbers and stuff one through that hole as quickly as possible. Once you open the sealed plastic, you are on the clock. Once the package of oxygen absorbers is opened, they begin to work right away as they are exposed to the oxygen in the air. If you work quickly,

. won't be a problem. It is just supposed to absorb the oxygen inside of the Mylar bag once it's sealed, so you need to get the next part done as quickly as possible.

After you've stuffed an oxygen absorber into each bag, you'll start with the first bag and bucket and push as much air out of the bag as possible, pull the bag back up, and using the board and iron, iron it shut the rest of the way.

Do this as quickly as possible for each of the bags and buckets that you have filled.

Once you've completed that, push the Mylar bag down into the bucket and place the lid on your bucket. You're done!

What Items Store Long Term?

We've covered so much in this chapter from enemies of food storage and how to defeat them, to how to repackage your food properly so that it will store for thirty years, not once have we mentioned what foods are safe to store thirty years if stored properly.

While this is in no wise a comprehensive list, the foods listed below are considered safe when stored properly:

Apple Cider Vinegar	Oats, Rolled
Beans, Dried Black	Pastas
Beans, Dried Kidney	Potato Flakes
Beans, Dried Navy	Salt
Beans, Dried Pinto	Sugar
Corn, Dried	Wheat Berries
Honey	White Rice
Milk, Powdered Non-fat	Vanilla
Oats, Quick	Grain Alcohol

If you want to know what foods are suggested to be stored for a year's worth of food, there are a lot of great food storage resources like this food storage calculator: http://www.thefoodguys.com/foodcalc.html. Make sure that you customize what it gives you for your family. If your family refuses to eat oats, don't store oats. If your family loves kidney beans, but refuses to touch soybeans, store more of one and less of the other.

So to recap, there are six different enemies to the long-term integrity of your food storage: light, oxygen, moisture, temperature, pests, and time. Storing your food is *not* a hard or time-consuming process, and there are plenty of foods that will keep for up to thirty years if stored properly.

While all of this is nice and important, I'd rather be talking about hot chocolate, biscuits with sausage gravy, sweet-and-sour chicken, and homemade macaroni and cheese. Wouldn't you? Well, in the next chapter we'll hit those as we discuss short-term food storage. All of those meals are possible with short-term food storage, and I'll show you how.

Chapter Three Assignments:

1. Find at least two grocery stores from which you can get your food storage buckets for free or at least really cheap.
2. Pick up five four- to six-gallon buckets, clean, disinfect, and dry them.
3. Purchase a set of five six-gallon Mylar bags and 2000 cc oxygen absorbers
4. Purchase a small number of twenty-five pound bags of long-term food storage items.

Properly bag your first set of long-term food storage items.

If you aren't sure where to find items mentioned in this chapter or you want my specific recommendations, you can find them listed in the Resource Center of the website:

https://www.ayearwithoutthegrocerystore.com/single-post/2017/12/07/Resource-Center

Chapter Four

Short-Term Food Storage

Think of food storage in general as your savings accounts. There are two types of savings accounts: general savings, and project savings, such as saving for a car or a home improvement project. A general savings account is your long-term food storage. Your project savings is like your short-term food storage. You always have a general savings account before you start saving for specific projects.

Starting with long-term food storage is your general safety net. Your project savings account is your short-term food storage. It allows you to eat comfort foods that your family loves, but it costs a little more and takes more time to gather.

Once you've taken care of the basics of long-term food storage, you can turn your attention to your short-term food storage. Did you know that the average American family wastes 25 percent of the food they purchase on a weekly basis?[4] If my family of seven is one of those typical households that's more than $3000 of food wasted each year. Those are no small peanuts. If you have a larger family, your potential savings is even more. So, in this chapter I'm going to show you how to save money on your short-term storage by planning a menu and the grocery list to go along with it. I'll also show you how to track the items in your pantry so that you know how much you have and how much you still need.

Steps to Short-Term Food Storage

The process is fairly simple. You're going to decide how many weeks' worth of food storage is your goal, choose meals, list the ingredients to the meals, set it up for the number of weeks you've chosen, create your grocery list, and start shopping.

But let's start simply: grab a spiral bound notebook or a three-ring binger.

---

[4] https://www.nrdc.org/sites/default/files/wasted-food-IP.pdf

How Long Will Your Short Term Storage last?

Take some time and think through how long you want your short-term storage to go for, remembering from Chapter Two that short-term food storage has two main purposes: to get you through a short-term crisis and to get you over the hump in a long-term crisis. How long of a short-term crisis do you feel it's necessary be prepared to get through, or how long do you think you'll need to adapt to a new circumstance with easily prepared foods?

In general, while most people shoot for three to six months of short-term storage, you can start with anything as short as a week. My minimum suggestion would be four weeks or a month. My maximum suggestion, starting out, would be three months. There are pros and cons to each choice. No matter how many weeks' worth of food storage you decide upon, just the act of making your decision is very important. Take the number of weeks you've decided on and write it on the inside cover of your spiral bound notebook or across top of the first page of your three-ring binder.

Favorite Meals

On page one, start by making a list of your favorite meals. If you have a family, ask each of them to suggest their five favorite meals.

It's that's simple—just choose five favorite meals per person or if you are by yourself, choose ten favorite breakfasts, ten lunches, and ten dinners.

Which Meals Work for Food Storage?

Once you have your list of meals, we'll move on to the next step to determine which meals would work well as a food storage meal. As I was working on my menu for next week, I asked my children to give me a suggestion for a meal to make this week. I had one say they wanted chili. Another said Sloppy Joes. One said tortilla soup. A fourth said meatloaf. Yet another said they wanted chicken pizza casserole.

Once you have that list of five favorite meals from everyone, I want you to look for a couple of common denominators that will help you determine if any of the suggestions you've been given will make helpful meals for food storage. Look for meals where most of the ingredients are dry, boxed, or canned goods and where the meal is *easy* to make.

In the example that I just gave, one of my children asked for chili as a meal this week. Well, chili is about as simple a meal as they come. The ingredients for our chili include three thirty-ounce cans of pinto beans, one #10 can of tomato sauce, chili seasoning, and two pounds of hamburger. Most of the ingredients are dry, boxed, or canned. The only thing that doesn't fit into that category is hamburger.

So the next question: is there a solution to having fresh ground beef to put into the chili or could I leave it out altogether and still have a decent meal? I actually have two options that would work. I can purchase #10 cans of freeze-dried ground beef. I could use two cups of freeze-dried beef in the recipe. I could also leave out the ground beef altogether, and have a meatless chili while still having lots of protein from the beans. Both work, so this would make an excellent food storage meal. When you find meals like that, put a star by them.

Another of my children asked for meatloaf. As much as I would try, meatloaf is not a meal that I am going to be able to make easily from food storage since the main ingredient in meatloaf is a fresh ingredient. This would not get a star added to my food storage meal list.

Go through the rest of the list of the meals suggested by your family and put a star by all of the ones that would be easily be able to be converted to food storage.

Seven of Breakfasts, Lunches, and Dinners

You're off to a great start! You've gone through a list of favorite meals to determine which could be easily made from food storage and put stars by those.

On page two of your notebook write "Breakfasts" at the top. Page three will be "lunches," and page four will be "dinners." You want to come up with seven breakfasts, lunches, and dinners that can be made from food storage. Why? Because this is the menu you're going to use for your food storage week by week. If you only have one week's menu that you repeat over and over, it simplifies things, while still giving you variety within your menu. We'll talk about that more later in the chapter.

As you're listing out your seven breakfasts, lunches, and dinners, don't always look for hard solutions. A couple of your breakfasts could be as simple as oatmeal or grits—both very easy meals to make with simple, dried ingredients. One of my kid's favorite meals, especially when we're in a crunch for time, is "Bean and Queso soup." The recipe is literally five cans of black beans, drained and rinsed, and a jar of queso. They rave about it. For dinners, soups are incredibly easy and oftentimes just require dumping the contents of cans or boxes into a pot or Crock-Pot and letting them simmer all day long. Remember, with short-term food storage, the ease of making your food is as important as having ingredients that are easily stored.

Once you've chosen your seven breakfasts, lunches, and dinners, this becomes your food storage menu. Think of this as your week. Look across the different pages where you have breakfast #1, lunch #1, and dinner #1. Those could be all the meals you'd eat on Sunday for breakfast, lunch, and dinner. Your #2 breakfast, lunch, and dinner could be eaten on Monday, etc. That makes things so much simpler for you.

Break the Ingredients Down By Meal

Give all your meals—all seven of your breakfasts, lunches, and dinners—each their own page in your notebook. Just write the meal at the top of the page. Once you've done that for all your meals, you need to write out *every* ingredient that you need to make that meal. I mean every ingredient, down to the spices. If one of my dinners was Tortilla Soup, I put Tortilla Soup at the top of the page. On the left-hand side of the page I would list:

2 black beans (canned)
2 corn (canned)
1-32 oz. chicken broth
2 chicken (canned)
1-30 oz tomato sauce
½ C taco seasoning mix

Once those amounts are listed on the left side of your page, go back to the inside cover and look at the number of weeks of food storage you've decided to have in your house. Since your seven breakfasts, seven lunches, and seven dinners represent one week's food storage. If you chose to start with four weeks of food storage, the easiest thing to do is to plan to make each of those meals four times—once per week.

What you'll do on each page is multiple the ingredients in each recipe by the number of weeks of food storage you already wrote on the top of page one. If you decided to start with four weeks of food storage, you're going to multiply each ingredient by four, so that it would look like this.

2 black beans	*8 black beans*
2 corn	*8 corn*
1-32 oz. chicken broth	*4-32oz chicken broth*
2 canned chicken	*8 canned chicken*
1-30 oz tomato sauce	*4-30 oz tomato sauce*
½ C taco seasoning mix	*2 C taco seasoning mix*

This gives you exactly what you'll need to make this meal four consecutive weeks. Let's say that you accomplish that goal. You can repeat this menu as often as you'd like. Personally, once I reach twelve weeks (approximately three months) of food storage, I start adding in new meals to the mix. I may only add two more breakfasts, lunches or dinners at a time, but I'll be expanding both my food storage and my menu so as not to get bored with the meals that we're making.

Once you have that list of ingredients written out, each time you go to the store, determine that you are going to pick up at least one or two food storage meals per week. If you feel like you need to get some food storage into your house quickly, you could even do a run just to pick up your food storage ingredients for as many meals as you feel you need.

Affordable food storage

When I look at my food storage menu, it can look daunting. To make meatless chili for the seven members of my family twelve times, costs me over $100. That's a lot of money. More than my grocery budget can afford to purchase in one week, let alone to purchase on *top* of my regular groceries each week. So how can a person afford food storage?

One way to afford food storage is to make purchases little by little. Start small. Maybe all your budget can afford is an extra ten to twenty dollars each week. Then purchase one or two food storage meals each time you to go the grocery store. It may only seem like a little, but that little will add up.

How can you purchase your short-term food most cost effectively? Some of these same areas overlap with where to get your long-term food storage.

Buy in bulk

Like your long-term food storage, Costco, Sam's Club, or BJ's Wholesale are definitely options for short-term food storage. There are different items that I purchase there, depending on whether I'm purchasing for long-term food storage or short-term food storage. While I may purchase #25 bags of rice for long-term food storage, I'll purchase a #10 (about a gallon) size cans of tomato sauce, a twelve-pack of six-ounce cans of tuna fish, freeze dried hash browns or many other items when I'm working on my short-term food storage.

Restaurant Supply Stores

Our local town has a store called Gordon's Food Service. It's a restaurant supply store from which anyone can purchase. This is an excellent place to get short-term food storage foods. Earlier in this chapter I mentioned that my children like "Bean and Queso soup." Well, I found that I could purchase a #10 size can of black beans for less than I could purchase five cans of black beans at many of our local grocery stores, and I get more in the can. Price and size makes this a better option for our short-term food storage. I've also seen larger, family size cans of soup for economical prices. They carry comfort foods like hot chocolate, pastas, #10 cans of country gravy, and so much more that are perfect for short-term food storage.

Purchase Online

When you start purchasing freeze-dried food, there are several economical ways to do it. My favorite way is to purchase through Thrive Life. You do have to purchase a membership—think of it like purchasing a

Costco or Sam's club membership. Once you do that, you can set up what they call a "Q." You set your budget, and you can either have them fill your cart monthly with foods that they suggest to you, or you can fill it yourself. Since my food storage is based around a menu, I always fill my cart myself.

A couple of the benefits to using Thrive Life is when I purchase over $100 of products on any given month, I earn a percent back and get free shipping on most things. I keep my Thrive Life purchases to items that I cannot easily buy elsewhere. My purchases usually consist of freeze-dried meats and cheeses. From time to time, I'll purchase specific fruits or vegetables, but those are generally cheaper when purchasing conventionally canned products.

Other companies out there that also sell freeze-dried foods include Auguson Farms, Emergency Essentials, and EFoods Direct. I would discourage you from buying great quantities of precombined freeze-dried meals in #10 cans like chicken à la king. Having some of these on hand can definitely make life easier (big plus), but they tend to cost a whole lot more than they would if you purchased the ingredients yourself. We have some of these, but we keep them to a minimum.

Your most costly investment in food storage will be meat. You can purchase freeze-dried meat. I have a good quantity of it around, but you can purchase other canned meats such as canned chicken, canned tuna, canned salmon, canned ham, or even sardines at very reasonable prices. Keep those in mind when you are building your food storage.

Another meat option is to obtain a pressure canner, and can your own meat. It is cheaper to purchase and cook your own ground beef and pressure-can it than it is to buy freeze-dried ground beef. Canning, whether water-bath canning or pressure-canning is beyond the scope of this book, but both of those things would be wise to know in order to economically add to your food storage.

Couponing

I've mentioned earlier in this book that I used to coupon. Well, if I were completely honest, that is the understatement of the year. I used to excel at couponing. I've walked out of CVS (a local drug store) earning more money than I spent. I've left a grocery store with twenty boxes of cereal and paid two dollars. It wasn't like that every week, but I fed a family of six on two hundred dollars a *month*. Not too shabby.

I took a hiatus from couponing after my youngest child was born. We weren't eating much boxed or canned goods. We were also transitioning away from the regular chemically laden household products and toiletries that you find in every grocery store. It was the right decision at the time.

When we wanted to get back to living more frugally within the last year, I started putting my couponing skills to work again to find out that couponing no longer works the way it used to work or as well as it used to work. Shows like *Extreme Couponing* made companies much wiser as to how coupons were being used or abused.

In my attempt to get back to couponing the way I had been five years prior, I was paying over seventy dollars a month to purchase coupon inserts, and I quickly learned that I wasn't saving seventy dollars a month in groceries, toiletries, and cleaning supplies.

It took some time and thinking our situation over, but I have come across the perfect way to coupon for my family and ensure that my family gets the greatest return on our money spent on coupons.

Each Wednesday when our grocery store ads come out, I go through the ad looking for the items my family regularly uses—canned goods, breads, prepackaged meats, boxed foods, toiletries, cleaning supplies, and the list could go on. I compare these items with the current coupons offered at www.klip2save.com. While there aren't current coupons for many of the items which are on sale that week, even two or three items which have coupons combined with an amazing sale make it worth my while.

As I compare the coupons with the store ads, I add any coupons to my cart for items that I wish to stock up on. This week alone, I got a seventy-five cent off coupon for toothpaste. I can get this toothpaste at one dollar a tube. When I combine this with a coupon, I will pay only twenty-five cents per tube of toothpaste. The coupons for the toothpaste only cost me eight cents a piece! I found shave gel on sale for $1.47. I found a corresponding coupon for one dollar off that shave gel. That means I'm only paying forty-seven cents for a container of shave gel. I pay the company "Klip2Save" for the time it takes them to clip the coupons I want and the fee to mail them to me. The coupons only cost me eight cents a piece. I purchase coupons for each member of my family, or if the deal is *that good*, I'll purchase ten or more coupons.

Using this technique to accumulate your food storage items will help you save more than all of the other ways put together.

Short-term food storage is the "fun" part of food storage. You get to choose foods your family loves for your menu. You can include comfort items such as hot chocolate, coffee, or tea. What's even better than that is that having this menu in place, you don't have to think about that elusive question, "What's for dinner?" because you'll already know! You'll also know that you have everything you need to make each of those delicious meals. While it is important to have food to eat if you hit demanding times or a power outage or a devastating storm, it's also important to be able to cook your food when these things happen.

Being able to obtain proper tools before you need them could be helpful on one hand or life saving on the other. Having premade kits put together and labeled for distinct types of emergencies is a time saver and saves trips to the grocery store or drug store if someone gets sick or you need to cook without power. All of these things and more will be discussed in Chapter 5.

Chapter Four Assignments:

1. Grab a notebook.
2. Decide how many weeks you want to begin with for your short-term food storage and list this on the inside cover or on the top of page one.
3. List five favorite meals from each family member. Put a star by any meals which will easily convert to food storage (boxed, canned, dried goods).
4. Choose seven breakfasts, seven lunches, and seven dinners. List them out in your notebook.
5. Give each recipe a page in your notebook, and write out all the ingredients for the meal.

6. Multiply the ingredients by the number of weeks of food storage you want to begin with.

7. Pick up the ingredients for at least two meals the next time you go to the grocery store.

If you aren't sure where to find items mentioned in this chapter or you want my specific recommendations, you can find them listed in the Resource Center of the website:

https://www.ayearwithoutthegrocerystore.com/single-post/2017/12/07/Resource-Center

Chapter Five
Food Storage Equipment, Tips, and Kits

"According to federal data, the U.S. electric grid loses power 285 percent more often than in 1984, when the data collection effort on blackouts began. That's costing American businesses as much as $150 billion per year, the DOE reported, with weather-related disruptions costing the most per event …

"Also, demand for electricity has grown 10 percent over the last decade, even though there are more energy-efficient products and buildings than ever. And as Americans rely increasingly on digital devices, summers get hotter (particularly in the southern regions of the U.S.) and seasonal demand for air conditioning grows, the problem is only getting worse."[5]

It's wintertime. You've worked on your long-term food storage, you've started getting your short-term food storage together. When you see on the weather forecast that your area is in the direct path of an ice storm, you don't panic because you have your food storage set up for plenty more than the three days that you would probably be affected.

You still don't panic when you wake up the next morning and find that the power is off to your entire neighborhood, but as you try to head to your basement to get to your food storage, you can't see because you can't find your flashlight. Then it dawns on you, food storage isn't any good if you don't have a way to cook it.

After racking your brains, you remember an old camp stove, but that would require you to cook out in the bitter cold since camp stoves can't be used indoors. You find a candle and miraculously remembered where you had some matches. You light it and head down to your basement to grab food, but you're not sure what to grab or where your camp stove is. You're

---

[5] http://www.lexingtoninstitute.org/wp-content/uploads/2016/09/Tomorrows-Electrical-Power-Grid.pdf

worried about the candle if you set it down so that you can use both of your hands to dislodge a box in which you think the camp stove is kept.

Things would have been so much easier if you had planned for more than food for your food storage.

Despite talking about food storage, I would be remiss if I didn't talk about ways to cook your food storage in an emergency. In this chapter, we're going to cover cooking meals from your food storage when you don't have electricity, tools and tips to make cooking your food storage easier, and kits that you can put together to make a power outage or other small emergency go much more smoothly.

Cooking Your Food Storage When the Power Is Down

So let's talk about cooking your food storage. Many of you already have ways that you could cook food if the power went out. You may just not have thought of them. Let's start with what most people already have.

1. Gas stovetop: Wait a minute, you said there's no power. Yep, but if you have a gas stove, you may still be in luck. Even if there's no power, if you have a match, you should still be able to cook on your gas stovetop. The only electric part to your stovetop is probably the ignition. You can safely light your gas cook top with a match. You'd simply turn on burner so that there is only a little gas coming out. Strike a match and hold it down near the burner. It should ignite. This gives you the ability to cook skillet meals, heat soup, and even heat water for coffee.

2. Gas Grill: Gas grills are wonderful for cooking up meat and even veggies, but did you know that in a pinch you can even bake in your gas grill? You will need to preheat your grill for ten to fifteen minutes, and then place your item(s) to be baked on your grill. Check them regularly, assuming that the temperature is around 350 degrees. If you are concerned or curious about what the temperature really is, you can purchase an inexpensive oven thermometer.

3. Camping Stove: If you have an electric household stove, then a decent second option is a camp stove. It works much like a traditional stovetop, so you can heat up soup, cook skillet meals or

do some pan-frying. The downside of a camp stove is that you can only use them outside or in an open area like a garage with the door open. These can't be used inside because they give off carbon monoxide.

4. Fire Pit: Even if you don't have a fire pit before you lose power, this is one thing (if you own your home) you could put in quickly to cook over. If you have or build a fire pit, having a grate that you can cook over it with is a "great" idea. You can grill, bake in a Dutch oven, heat a soup, or cook over the open fire. There's a lot of potential with a fire pit.

5. Butane stove: Amazon has several single burner butane stoves. We have one with several canisters of butane. If our gas stove isn't working, we can pull out our butane stove. It gives us many of the same options as our gas stovetop does. I have read that this is safe to cook with indoors, and also that it is not. No matter what you choose, make sure you have a good carbon monoxide detector in your house.

6. Saratoga Jack: Ever considered a Crock-Pot that doesn't require gas or electricity? Well in a nutshell, that's what a Saratoga Jack does. You start by heating the liquid contents of the Saratoga's pot to the boiling point. You then slip that pot into your Saratoga Jack, close the lid, and voilà, you have a Crock-Pot that doesn't require electricity. The Saratoga Jack will keep the food cooking and hot for up to twelve hours after putting the insert inside and closing the lid. If you have an electric stove, but you want to invest in a butane stove and a Saratoga Jack, and then you can cook almost anything.

7. HERC Oven: A HERC oven is an oven heated by tea lights. It might sound odd, but in an enclosed area, tea lights give off enough heat that you can bake. A HERC oven is designed to harness that heat and channel it into baking. While I'm not sure I'd want to bake a chicken in a HERC oven, it should be good enough for baked goods like biscuits, brownies, cookies, oven pancakes, etc. While a buying HERC oven may be expensive, with a little know how, you can make one yourself for forty dollars or less.

8. Wood Stove: There are some definite advantages to having a wo stove. It will heat your house. You can cook on top of it, and if you get the right wood stove, you can even bake in it. I highly recommend the Vermont Bun Baker wood stove. This is the one we have. You can cook on the top and bake in the bottom, heat your house with it, and potentially even have hot water using it.

9. Solar Oven: With a solar over, you can bake using only the sun's rays. Just keep in mind, it is much harder to bake when it's cold outside. But with a solar oven, you could potentially bake a chicken. They aren't much cheaper than buying a HERC oven, but you can use them for more than you can a HERC oven.

Since we're discussing cooking without power, I want to highlight some tools that will be invaluable if you are without power. These are things that you won't likely need in a power outage, but if something would happen to knock out the power for a considerable length of time, these will be very helpful.

The year my youngest child was born, we were at a Good Friday church service in small town about an hour and a half from our home in Ferguson, Missouri. At the time, my husband was a bi-vocational pastor. In other words, he worked a regular nine-to-five job during the week and pastored on the weekend. At the end of the service, just before my husband started praying, my phone rang. I quickly silenced it. It rang again. I turned it off. When the service was over, I turned the phone on and found a call from my mom. I called her back, and she was panicked beyond words. She needed to make sure we were all okay. While my husband was preaching in Bowling Green, Missouri, our house had been struck by a tornado. They needed to know we were safe.

It took three hours that night to make what was usually a one-and-a-half-hour drive home. When we arrived in our small suburb of St. Louis, our street was one of the ones that had been cordoned off. We couldn't even walk to our house to get items that we needed for an overnight. We learned several lessons here.

First off, your car should always have a kit with basics for food for your family for a minimum of twenty-four hours. This kit should also have items for personal hygiene in it and one change of undergarments for everyone. We would have stunk a whole lot less the next day with those items and we wouldn't have had to unexpectedly eat out.

Twenty-four hours later, we were able to get back into our house which was standing, but greatly damaged. Having seventy-two hour kits was so helpful. While my husband and I were contacting our insurance company and repair companies to get things get into motion, we all had clothes, hygiene items, and the kids had activities in their packs. We picked up my computer and a few more of our movies, and headed to the hotel in which our insurance company put us up for the time being. Not having to scrounge around in debris for a clean change of clothes or to have to purchase completely new toiletries or things for our kids to do was so helpful. We were without water, gas, and electricity in our house for over a week. These things happen, and can happen to anyone.

So let's look at tools that we need to consider. Learning to cook with your food storage is a must before anything little or big happens. Everything you do before there are hard times gives you the confidence that you could do it again if times got hard. If you have used a grain mill before times got tough, you're not going to worry about grinding grain after an event. If you have taken the time to learn how to pressure-can food before hard times strike, you're going to feel so much more at home if you have to pressure-can something after any type of event.

Let's keep in mind practice is the key, so how can we practice and prepare before an event? Each week, plan one meal that you will cook using an alternate method. Try to incorporate some of the items below as you acquire them so that you can practice how to use them and feel confident when you have to use them after an emergency.

1. Manual can opener: Many people use electric can openers. If you are one of these people, one of the first things you need to purchase is a manual can opener.

2. Hand-crank grain grinder: The Deluxe grain mill by Victorio is a decent quality starter grinder that will grind wheat, corn, or other grains. If the power goes down and you want to bake bread or other bread-type products, you'll need a way to grind your wheat. You can also use ground wheat in cream of wheat breakfast cereal.

You can grind corn and make it into grits. With the Victorio, you might have to grind the corn twice to get the consistency for corn meal or grits. The Family Grain Grinder is a great mid-level grinder. If you are looking for more of a high-end grain mill, I would suggest that Country Living Grain Mill.

3. Eggbeaters: in the absence of power, the best way to mix foods fairly easily is an old-fashioned eggbeater. This won't do stiff doughs or batters like bread dough or cookie dough, but they will work in a pinch to mix either dry or liquid ingredients.

4. Whisk: Besides eggbeaters, a good whisk will go a long way to helping you in the kitchen. A whisk can be used to whip egg whites to peaks, to whip cream, or to mix dry items together well for your recipes.

5. A hand chopper: One like Pampered Chef's Food Chopper will work really well in cutting down on your prep time for chopping vegetables. Along those lines, I have found a hand crank mini-food processor that would also work well in cutting fruits and vegetables.

6. A good set of knives is invaluable. You can do almost anything with them. If you feel like you can't afford some of these items then a good set of knives will also work, it will just take longer.

7. Mandolin and glove: I consider these as going together. If you are going to have a mandolin for slicing fruits or veggies, you will need a cut-proof glove. The last thing you need if you are in the midst of an emergency is a severe cut on your hand or finger. If you have the mandolin, please invest in a cut-proof glove.

8. Hand-crank coffee grinder: I was surprised how long it took me to grind enough coffee to make a "pot" when we were without electricity, but life called for coffee. While the two or three minutes of turning the crank was a bit onerous, it was well worth it for hot coffee on a powerless morning.

9. French Press: This is an excellent way to make coffee without power. You put the coffee grounds into the bottom of the French press. You insert the plunger piece toward the top of the French press pot, pour hot water in about one third of the way full. Let it sit for three to four minutes, then fill the press with water. You

slowly press the press's plunger down through the water trapping all the coffee grounds at the bottom of the press, then you can pour out two to four nice, hot cups of coffee.

10. Water-bath canner: You can use a water-bath canner to can highly acidic foods—mostly fruits. You can make jams or jellies and use your water-bath canner to preserve them.

11. Pressure canner: While a water-bath canner is used with only highly acidic foods, a pressure canner can be used to preserve most kinds of foods. Because the pressure in a pressure canner produces temperatures higher than 212 degrees Fahrenheit, it can kill germs, mold, and toxins that would still thrive if you were using a water-bath canner.

12. Berkey Water Filter: The best water filter around is a Berkey Water Filter. It is capable of filtering out 99.999 percent of any bacteria in water and 99.99 percent of viruses in water. Our family uses our Berkey water filter daily—we don't wait for an emergency to take advantage of a filter that will get rid of the chlorine and fluoride out of the water that we drink daily.

Preparedness kits

There are many different types of preparedness kits such as a Bug Out Bag (BOB), a Get Home Bag, a Seventy-Two-Hour kit, a car kit, and the list goes on. I'm going to take some time to discuss different kits and the food that in contained within them. These may be part of larger kits, like a Seventy-Two-Hour kit, or a car kit, but the food aspect is very important. The reason that it is important to take time to put kits together is that if the power goes out, you've got everything that you could possibly need together in one tote, which will make life so much easier for you and your family. Having each of these kits will take so much pressure off of you in a crisis. It will turn things from more than chaotic into an inconvenience—at least for a couple of days.

Car Kits

The purpose of a car kit is to help you be prepared in case you are out and about, and you get stranded. This kit is supposed to help you get home if a repair or contacting someone isn't possible. While that may be the ultimate purpose of a car kit, we've used our car kits on normal days as well. When we went to an outdoor wedding rehearsal, we were being eaten alive by mosquitoes. I headed back to our van and pulled out some of our homemade bug spray. It did the trick. We were out in the sun longer than we expected, so we pulled out some of our sunscreen too. Get caught in an unplanned rain shower? Pull out your umbrella. Your morning trip takes longer than you planned? Pull out snacks from your snack box.

While I'll list other things that should be found in your car kit, I'd like to spend some time on the food portion. The purpose of the food portion of your car kit is in case you get stranded and you can't get home or to a place where you can get food right away. It's also a great option for us because, as a homeschool family, we do a lot of running around. If we're out longer than we anticipate and my kids get hungry, we have our food kit. I've been asked on more than one occasion by my kids if they can have a snack from our food kit. Sometimes the answer is "Yes," other times the answer is "No." But no matter what the answer is, we have the food and drinks for emergencies whether they are great or small.

Obviously, you need portable food. You also need food that will stay shelf-stable even at hot temperatures. The food in your car kit should be mostly protein and carbohydrates, but having some sugar for quick energy is also helpful.

Ideas for your food kit for your car—single servings are best for all the following:

Trail mix
Nut packs
Tuna fish pouches with
	spoons
Cheese crackers
Peanut butter crackers
Meat sticks
Granola bars
Cheese and cracker sticks
Peanut butter singles
Hard candies

Peppermints (for nausea as
	well as energy)
Sunflower seeds
Freeze-dried fruits or
	vegetables
Beef Jerky
Juice boxes (Water bottles
	can freeze in the cold or
	leach chemicals in the
	heat)

Other items for your car kit:

Map	Trash-can liners
Walking shoes	Gallon Size Ziploc bags
Feminine Hygiene supplies	First aid kit
Ponchos (one for each member of your family)	Umbrella
	Toilet paper
Jumper cables	Fire starter kit
2 phone chargers	Berkey water bottle
Bug spray	Headlamp
Sunburn care	Hand warmers
A book to read	Rescue blankets
A game to play	First Aid kit
Knife	Blankets
Basic sewing kit	Emergency Radio
Sharpie	Crank flashlight
Pen	Small roll duct tape
Pad of paper	Work gloves
Baby wipes	Tarps

Seventy-Two-Hour Kit

A second type of kit that is helpful to have is a seventy-two-hour kit or a Bug Out Bag. Each Bug Out Bag should be equipped with seventy-two hours worth of food. The purpose of the kit is to get you through the first seventy-two hours of a crisis. Instead of packing three days' worth of food into each person's bag, it made more sense for us to keep all the food together in one container. We keep our food in a short tote in case we need to leave in the event of an emergency. If we do have to leave, at least wherever we go, we will be bringing three days of food for us.

This is one time that we spend more on convenience foods. Oatmeal packets are our breakfast for all three days. We do two packets per person since most of my kids would feel incredibly hungry with only one. For lunch, we have one day of Mac and Cheese, to which I'll add a can of chicken and two days of tuna fish, crackers, and freeze-dried fruits. For dinners, we have three different dried soup mixes that just need water.

For your family, choose three breakfasts, lunches, and dinners. You could have the same thing every breakfast, lunch, or dinner just for simplicity sake. Set these items aside. A tote would be most ideal, but even if you start with them in secured grocery bags and know where they are, you'll be ahead of the game. Include paper products, plates, bowls, spoons, knives, forks, and napkins or paper towels. Don't forget you'll need water. Plan for one gallon per person, per day for drinking, cooking, and hygiene purposes. Also don't forget to put at least one can opener in your kit.

Simple Options for Breakfast

Oatmeal

Grits

Cold cereal

Granola Bars

Boxed Pastries

Freeze dried hash browns

Hot chocolate

Instant Coffee or regular
  coffee if you have a
  French press

Tang or orange drink
  equivalent.

Simple Lunch or Dinner Options

Crackers and meat (potted
  deviled ham, turkey, or
  chicken or canned tuna
  fish or salmon)

Macaroni and Cheese

Spam and beans

Beans and Rice

Canned Soups

Sandwiches

Spaghetti

Boxed Dinners such as Tuna
  Helper

Canned Pasta

Soup and Rice

Salmon Patties

Tuna Patties

Other items helpful to be in your Bug Out Bag are
Clothes:

One to two changes of
  clothes,

Hygiene baggie a quart size
  baggie containing:

Soap

Travel shampoo

Travel deodorant

Wash cloth

Comb

Hair bands (for ladies)

Feminine products (for
ladies)

Travel size package of hand
wipes

Mini Kleenex

Toothbrush

Travel size toothpaste

Baby powder

Lotion, floss

Travel Q-tips

First Aid kit

Travel Help:

Headlamp

Knife

Leatherman

Cigarette lighter

Waterproof matches

Work Gloves

Two-person tent

Two bandanas

For Kids

Something fun to do

A "lovie" or stuffed animal

Power Outage Kits

Our seventy-two-hour food tote doubles as our food for a power outage. The difference is that we have a very large (twenty-seven gallon) tote set aside simply as a power outage kit for everything outside of the kitchen. We have another twenty-seven-gallon tote with all the items we use to cook when the power is out if we are staying home.

Since our food kit is the same, I'm going to list off the items in our cooking kit:

Single burner butane stove

Butane canisters

Matches

Eggbeaters

Hand crank mini food
processor

Can openers

French press coffee pot

Hand crank coffee grinder

Hand chopper

Hand crank grain grinder

Multiple sources of lighting
(ya gotta see to cook)

Sickness Kit

This is something that many people overlook. If one of your family members comes down with the stomach flu in the middle of the night, the last thing you want to do is to have to run to the store and pick up food and drinks appropriate to the sickness. Having these things set aside ahead of time will give you peace if someone gets sick normally, but imagine someone getting sick in the middle of an ice storm with you not being able to venture outside your home. This could be the difference between comfort and panic.

In our sickness tote we keep:

Crackers	Peppermint tea
Cans of chicken noodle soup	Nausea medicines
Jars of applesauce	Fever medicines
Chicken broth	Cold and Flu medicines
Lemon-Lime soda	

Once you start getting these totes in order, you're going to need to figure out how to organize all of them! In Chapter Six, we're going to talk about how to organize your food storage and your kits. I'll walk you through how our food storage started in one small cabinet and grew to the room we have now. We'll give you tips and tricks if you live in an apartment or a small space, and we'll talk about places that you want to avoid keeping your food storage.

Chapter Five Assignments:

1. Start working on your sickness kit first. This is the one you'll probably use more often than the other kits.
2. Pick three ways to cook during a power outage. Make sure you're set up to cook all three ways.
3. Look through the list of kitchen tools or ways to cook that you want to acquire and number them from most important to least important. Buy whatever item is currently #1 as you are able.
4. Create your menu for the food portion of your seventy-two-hour kit and power outage kit. Start picking things up as you make grocery trips.

If you aren't sure where to find items mentioned in this chapter or you want my specific recommendations, you can find them listed in the Resource Center of the website:

https://www.ayearwithoutthegrocerystore.com/single-post/2017/12/07/Resource-Center

Chapter Six
Organizing and Tracking Your Food Storage

In 1973, the average family size was 3.01 persons per household, and the average size of a home was 1,660 square feet. By 2014, things had changed. The average household size had shrunk to 2.54 persons per household, but the average house size has grown to 2,690 square feet. "The average living space per person has almost doubled in just the last 41 years."[6] I'm not going to get into what this is saying about our country and how we are making decisions about our family size or the size of our house or even how many possessions anyone has, but I will say that at least bodes well for how much space you can likely find in your home for food storage.

As a homeschooling mom, hardly a day goes by in our house where I don't hear one of the kids say something along the lines of, "Mom, I can't find my …" Fill in the blank. It might be a pencil, their schoolbook, a protractor, you name it. Someone is not going to be able to find something that they need to complete their school for the day.

Even if your kids go to school, I'm sure it's the same way. "Mom, I can't find my …" Maybe it's science homework or a grammar book, or a red pen. It is very hard to keep track of things that are not kept in specific places. Even when things are kept in specific places, if people don't put things back in specific places assigned, things are hard to track.

As we start to talk about finding places for our food storage or organizing our food storage, I want to give you an example of why having a place to put your food storage is important.

A couple of months ago, I was looking for duct tape in our house. I needed to use it for a project and it wasn't in the place that I normally kept it. I have five children. In having five children, it means that sometimes my children take things for family use or my use. I looked all over and couldn't find it. I ended up picking up a four pack of duct tape on Amazon. I stashed the four rolls around the house in different places, that way if they

---

[6] https://www.census.gov/construction/chars/pdf/c25-7713.pdf
https://www.census.gov/construction/chars/completed.html

found one of the rolls they wouldn't necessarily find the rest of them. The problem with that is that I didn't write down where I put my duct tape. Because I didn't write it down, I can only remember where one of those rolls of duct tape is. The same goes for your food storage. If you have no idea where your food storage is, it's going to do you absolutely no good when you go to use it.

Start Small

You've heard the saying, "A place for everything and everything in its place." That is so apropos here. When we first started collecting food storage in our house close to ten years ago, I had just started couponing. I started really small. As I learned how to coupon, I started to collect food, toiletries, cleaning products, and paper products. It wasn't just to hoard the food. We used everything we collected.

I needed to find a place to put the extra food and supplies because we really didn't have a pantry to speak of in our house. I walked through our house with new eyes, specifically looking for places that we could put our food. During that walk through, I realized that I couldn't put everything in one location. I started by putting canned goods in an unused cabinet in our garage. I couldn't put our glass jars out there or boxed goods in case critters got into the garage, but it was something. It worked well for a little bit.

After that I realized that I needed some more space. I cleared off one of the easily accessible shelves in our garage to keep some other things like paper products. I could also put out larger canned goods than would fit into our garage cabinet. Then when we outgrew that space, and I started looking for other spaces that we could start keeping things. We installed bed risers under our to expanded our food storage to the space beneath it. We realized that there were several shelves in our bedroom closet that could house items. We kept all our toothpaste, mouthwash, floss, Band Aids, and first aid supplies in there.

We went to the local Latter-day Saints cannery and made the bulk foods purchase I mentioned in Chapters Two and Three, and put all the dry goods we purchased into Mylar and sealed the bags in five-gallon buckets. We used these buckets in place of box springs for a bed. Because we used a dust ruffle on the bed, no one ever knew that we had buckets as our boxed springs. We finally got to the point where we decided that to consolidate some children and bedrooms, and to use one of the bedrooms as a food storage room. We had three large shelving units in the ten by twelve-foot bedroom, and we filled them all. Between canned goods and boxed goods, between paper products and cleaning products, between our five-gallon buckets and some limited equipment we had picked up, we filled that room. When it came time for use to move, some of our food storage got sold; some of it moved with us.

When we moved out of Ferguson, we moved from an 1,800 square-foot house to an 1,100 square foot house, and we moved with some of our food storage. We had to find a way to store our food again. Our food storage had taken a whole room, and now we didn't have a whole room in which to put it.

What I want you to understand from this story is you don't need to worry up front about where you're going to put three months' worth of food storage. All you need to do is to decide where you are going to put one month's worth of food (if that's your first goal). That's not as big of a deal as six months or more. When you get to the place where you're getting ready to store twelve weeks' worth of food, that takes more space, but you don't have to start there.

The thing I want to impress upon you as you start this chapter is you need to start small.

Where Can I Find Space and Six Questions

Walk through your house and look for places that you don't use. Go through each room with new eyes, asking yourself, "What are the spaces in this room? Are there spaces in this room I can use? If not, are there items that I can consolidate together to free up some space?"

1. Can I store my stash *under* something? A great example of this is under our bed. When we moved from the 1,800 square-foot house to the 1,100 square-foot one, we had to get creative with our space. We used risers to raise our bed so we could fit food storage items and gallon jugs of water under it. Another example is using buckets in place of a bed frame and box spring mattress.

2. Can I store items *in* something? Do you have a hollow ottoman? That's a place where you can store things. We have put bookcases in our closets on a couple of occasions in order to store items in our closet where it wouldn't be an eyesore.

3. Can I store things *out in the open*? We like to keep our oil lamps out since they are decorative. In our 1,100 square-foot house, we would store some of our food in half-gallon jars on top of the cabinets. With the different colors and textures, it looked decorative.

4. Can I store items *behind* something? Do you have a couch that could be pulled eight to twelve inches away from the wall so that you could put a thin table behind it? If so, you could store some of your food under that table, between your couch and the wall.

5. Can I store items in *rooms* I've not considered using before? Can you consolidate some children so you can have a whole room for food storage? I have had one of my children who gave up her own room in order for us to have that room for food storage thank me more than once for making sure she would be taken care of if something happened and we couldn't go grocery shopping. Her sister, on the other hand was overjoyed that they would be sharing a room. She didn't like being on her own. Maybe you have an office? Could you consider giving up even a wall of your office if you couldn't give up the whole thing?

6. Can I move items to a *new space* and take over the *old space* for storage? If you're like me, you may have an overabundance of towels. What if you kept one towel for each member of your family and put up one hook for each person on the back of their doors? That would free up much (if not all) if your linen closet space.

These six questions can come in very handy as you're going through your home to find space for your storage.

You've made a point to start small. You've decided where you are going to start stashing your food storage. Now you need to organize your food by type.

Organizing by Types of Items

Buckets: We kept all our buckets together. This is our long-term food storage. It makes good sense to keep them all together.

Canned goods: Because of the plethora of canned goods that we have, we would further break this type down into proteins, fruits, vegetables, soups, and sauces. We would make sure that all of our proteins were kept together, so that when we needed a can of something that falls under the heading of protein, we know where to look for it.

Spices and flavorings: Look for a cool dry place to keep these. You don't want moisture making your spices clump.

Equipment: I keep my equipment organized so I know where to look when it comes time to water-bath can my apple butter or apple sauce, or when I need Crock-Pot #2 or #3, or even where to find my extra Berkey filters.

Water: We've learned some valuable lessons about storing water over the years. When we put our bed up on risers, we would store gallon jugs of water under the bed in short totes. There was enough room that we had three to six inches of clearance. What we didn't take into consideration was that our kids would come in and pounce on our bed. From time to time when a child would do that, one of the gallon water jugs would have the top compressed and would burst a seam in the plastic. Storing water under beds isn't necessarily the best idea. The best place to store water is in the basement, if you have one. If you don't have a basement, find a dark place with consistent cool or room temperature.

Drinks: We store coffee, tea, hot chocolate, and drink mixes together.

Personal Care Products: Your pantry should include personal care products. Keep these grouped together either by the whole category or by type, like toothpaste and anything else dealing with teeth, anything dealing with hair and body, deodorant, etc.

Cleaning Products: Always having backups of your cleaning products is very important besides being incredibly efficient. Keep these together and in a place that's out of reach of small children.

First Aid Products: Have first aid and over the counter products on hand. You don't want to be running out to the local drug store when the stomach flues, or fevers, or sore throats hit. Keep these types of things in an out of the reach place. Also make sure that you are checking expiration dates regularly.

Paper products: We try to keep all our paper products in one place. We keep an extra or two in places where we use it most often. For example, we keep a large pack of toilet paper in the bottom of our linen closet, but we keep the vast majority of it with the rest of our stored paper products.

Whether you are keeping categories in different places across your home or in one room, you're going to know exactly where they are if you are keeping them organized by category.

Keeping in Mind Shelf-Life When Organizing, a.k.a. Rotating Your Food

Canned goods are labeled with an expiration date. Sticking with the date printed on the can is the safest way to handle canned goods. There are times that I will eat foods past their listed expiration dates, but I'm not saying that you should. Without looking at each individual can, how can you know what foods that you have that are the oldest?

There is a system that you can set up called FIFO—First In, First Out. These are racks in which you put your canned goods in the top slot and you remove your canned goods from the bottom of the slot. If you pay attention to the canned soup dispensers in most stores, you'll see what I'm talking about. The store clerk will put the soups in the slot on the top. That soup will roll down until it hits the last can of soup. As you remove a can of soup from the bottom, then all the cans of soup slide down one space.

There are FIFO organizers out there for soup size cans, for #10 size cans and everything in between. This is the simplest way to make sure that you use your food in the order that you bought your food.

If you can't afford FIFO can systems, you can always write the month and year that you purchased them on the top of the can and use the flat of cans from the bottom of the pile first.

In our house, we keep all our canned goods in flats. We buy most of our canned goods (especially the food we buy for food storage) by the flat. The oldest flat is on the bottom of the pile. The newest flat goes on the top. When we are ready to use our canned goods, we pull the oldest flat from the bottom, put it on top and mark the top of each can with an "X." 'l lets us know that this is the flat from which we're supposed to pull. rotates our stock with very little difficulty.

Organizing on Paper or Electronically

You've started small. You found creative places to put your food. You organized your items by type, and you started rotating your items. Now one step further is knowing how much food is in your house at any given time.

There are two very simple ways to go about this. The fastest way to organize your personal storage is on paper. You've already organized your storage into categories. Get a notebook or a clipboard and start with a page per category. List off your items (black beans, toothpaste, and anything in between) and put a tally for each can or box or unit you have of each. After the name of the item, make sure that you write down where that type of food is found if you don't keep all your food in the same location

Once you've taken inventory of what's in your house, you can go to your food storage that you listed off earlier in the book and see what you have for each recipe and what you still need. This gives you the next steps on your next grocery list. If you have tomato sauce for chili, but you don't have any beans, then you know what to pick up next.

An easier way to organize things in the long term is electronically with a spreadsheet. Here's an example of one meal from my spreadsheet.

Meal #	Meal	Components	Needed for 1	Needed for 12	Have	Running Tally
1	Mexica le Pie	Black Beans (in 15 oz cans)	3 cans	36	62	26
		Pinto Beans (in 30 oz cans)	1 cans	12	62	50
		Chili beans (in 15 oz cans)	1	12	39	27
		Dry Milk	⅔ C	8	105	97
		Queso	1 jar	12	12	0
		Rice	3 C	36	179	143
		Dried Eggs	2	24	658	634
		FD Beef	1 C	12	50	38

l spreadsheet program and listed all of my meals down
ve, you'll see Meal # 1 is Mexicale Pie. I broke the meal up
ponent ingredients and amounts that I need to make it once,
goal is to be able to make all my meals twelve times so that I have
months worth of short-term food storage. The next column, then, is
what I need for one meal twelve times. So to make Mexicale Pie twelve
times, I need thirty-six cans of black beans. The next column is how many
cans of black beans I actually have in my house. The running tally is the
number I have minus the number I need. So if I need to use black beans in
another recipe, then I know what number to put in the "Have" line of the
next recipe.

Ingredients	Have	Need
Baking Powder (in cups)	3	2 ¾
Basil	5	1.5
Black Beans	62	-10
Bean Soup Mix (in cups)	144	72
Beef, FD	50	-10
butter powder	12	4.5
Carrots, FD	12	0

If you know how to work a spreadsheet program, you can make it work
for you. I worked my spreadsheet to let me put in how many cans of black
beans or cups of baking powder. Then it automatically takes that number
and puts it in the "Have" slot for the next place that item is listed on my
spreadsheet. The "Running Tally" goes to the next recipe which contains
the same item, and once I don't have any more of that item in any of my
recipes, my spreadsheet tells me how much more I need to complete my
three months of short-term food storage or how much I have left over.

So looking at what I have above, I still need ten cans of black beans and
ten cups of freeze-dried beef, but I have more baking powder, basil, bean
soup mix, butter powder, and freeze-dried carrots than I need. So I know
the next time I go to the store, I need to pick up black beans, and on my
next Thrive Life order, I need an additional can of freeze-dried beef.

All of this may sound wonderful, but some of you out there might have
issues with certain food, or have children who have issues with certain

foods. In our house, we have one who can't have gluten or sugar. I know other people have problems with dairy or eggs. Some people chose to eat Paleo, and realize that's a choice that wouldn't necessarily continue if they fell into an economic hardship. Even though that is true, they know that they feel so much better when they eat that way. There are vegetarians and vegans out there who would want to store food in accordance with that preference. The next chapter is all about how to handle food storage if you have dietary issues.

Chapter Six Assignments:

1. Don't stress and start small.
2. Walk through your house to see where you can stash your food storage.
3. Organize your items by type and decide where each type is going to go.
4. Develop your plan for rotating your first aid supplies and food storage items.
5. Decide how to organize your storage on paper or electronically.

If you aren't sure where to find items mentioned in this chapter or you want my specific recommendations, you can find them listed in the Resource Center of the website: https://www.ayearwithoutthegrocerystore.com/single-post/2017/12/07/Resource-Center

Chapter Seven
Specialized Diets

Over the last ten years the incidence in childhood food allergies has increased approximately eighteen percent in children under 18 years of age[7].

My own personal experience has definitely verified this on a non-scientific level. The number of people in my life who has been on specialty diets because of food allergies or intolerances is startlingly high.

Our family has been on specialized diets both for myself and for some of my children. I can tell you that they can be hard enough at normal times, but during hard times they look impossible. I want to take some of the mystery out of specialized diets for you as you consider putting together your food storage.

One of the interesting things I realized was that there is a lot of overlap between some of the specialty items needed for different diets. For example, the milk and cheese alternatives for the dairy-free diet also work for a vegan diet. The same holds true with the egg-free diet and the vegan diets.

So let's delve into problem solving for different diets.

Gluten Free

I am probably most familiar with a gluten free diet. I have one son on a gluten free diet right now. His sister had to be on a gluten free diet for a couple of years, but we helped her gut heal to the point that it is no longer an issue for her.

The challenge with a gluten free diet is that you can't cook or bake with regular flours or use wheat in any form. For those who aren't familiar with the diet, that might not seem like a lot until you realize that wheat seems to be in almost everything.

There are several ways to adapt your diet for long-term food storage.

---

[7] Branum AM, Lukacs SL. Food allergy among U.S. children: Trends in prevalence and hospitalizations. NCHS data brief, no 10. Hyattsville, MD: National Center for Health Statistics. 2008

Let's start by exploring alternative gluten free flours. I would highly suggest flour alternatives that have a 1:1 ratio with regular flour. This will be the easiest way for you to transition to a gluten free-based food storage diet. No matter what you have in your pantry, you're going to have to learn how to make your own bread, so that's not a challenge you wouldn't have to face anyway. The two best alternative flours that I've discovered are Thrive Life's gluten free flour and Bob's Red Mill gluten free flour. Thrive Life's cost for the gluten free flour is very reasonable. I find the flour works well for my purposes. Bob's Red Mill also has a 1:1 gluten free flour that works well, but it is much more expensive.

There are recipes out there by which you can make your own gluten free flours, but the issue with many of those is that they use almond flour or coconut flour which goes rancid quickly—not a good idea when you are looking at long term food storage.

Another option is to use regular flour and ferment it into sour dough. If your doctor has told you never to touch gluten, this is not an option for you. If, however, going gluten free is something you are experimenting with on your own, this might be something for you to try. Flours can be soaked overnight. I'm not going to go into the whole process here, but if you do some research on soaking your flour or your wheat berries, it could be another easier (and less expensive) way for you to go about dealing with the problems that gluten causes for many people with gut issues.

Even if I was using gluten free flour or soaked flours, there are items that I would never likely make on my own or at best I wouldn't make them often—items like noodles and pasta. If you are looking for a fairly low-cost alternative for these types of items, which can be a staple in some food storage pantries, Aldi carries a "Live G Free" brand of pastas in various types. Just keep an eye on the expiration dates.

Paleo

This diet is generally a lifestyle choice. If you get to the point where you need to eat from your food storage pantry, it might be the time to not worry about eating exclusively Paleo. If you choose to do so anyway, it isn't impossible, just more expensive.

The most expensive part of eating Paleo is the meat. I'm currently paying about fifty dollars for ten cups of freeze dried meat. Keep in mind when you add water to the meat, it does expand. Even at that, I limit myself to one cup of meat per meal for my family. I just can't justify more cost for food storage. One cup of rehydrated freeze-dried meat is the approximate equivalent to one pound of meat.

There is another option though. As is always the case, what you gain in cost, you will sacrifice in time. Pressure-canning meat is a great alternative to using freeze-dried meat. We don't usually think of pressure-canning meat, because we don't usually see meats in the stores that are pressure-canned (maybe besides tuna, salmon, and chicken). Meats can be pressure-canned, and there are plenty of books and groups out there that will help you learn to pressure-can.

Another issue with the Paleo diet is having adequate vegetables. This is where a big garden comes into play. Having a garden will supply you with food to last you the growing season, and if you grow enough food, you can preserve it for the rest of the year using water-bath or pressure-canning. Gardening is a skill that must be learned and the sooner you start learning, the better. Most of your vegetables will also need to be pressure-canned, so that is another skill you will need to learn.

For the off-season, you can even propagate many foods indoors from scraps. These include celery, romaine lettuce, chives, garlic, basil, mint, onion, tomato, pineapple, and I'm sure there are others. You could work on an indoor garden for wintertime.

Fortunately there are other, less difficult options for the short term. Canned vegetables are prevalent and are not incredibly expensive. Picking them up at the store is a no-brainer.

Another option for your vegetables is getting them freeze-dried. I can get freeze-dried vegetables from Thrive Life for a very reasonable price. They can be purchased either in #10 family-size cans or in Pantry cans, which hold about a quart.

Most people store sugar as their sweetener of choice for long term food storage, but that's not allowed on the Paleo diet. There are two sweeteners that are allowed on (a non-strict) version of the diet that store very well—maple syrup and honey. Not only does honey store incredibly well, it can be used in your first aid regimen as well. I have found very good prices on maple syrup and honey at Costco and wonderful prices on quality honey through Azure Standard. If I had to choose between Azure and Costco on quality for honey, I would choose Azure, though of course Costco's prices are better.

Flours that work with Paleo are the hardest thing to substitute because the flours allowed on Paleo—almond flour and coconut flour—do not keep for long. Almond flour keeps for six months in the fridge and six more months if you keep it in the freezer, but for long-term food storage, neither the fridge nor the freezer is promised to be a part of the equation. Coconut flour will last for six months in the fridge and another year in the freezer.

For long-term food storage, those adhering to the Paleo diet should not count on storing flours to bake things.

Dairy Free

Non-dairy milk replacement

I think one of the most difficult items to swap out is milk. I've made milk substitutes before from coconut and from almonds, but neither of those stores well long term. Oats, however, do store well long term, and they make a creamy replacement for milk.

All you need is:

1 cup oats
4–5 cups hot water
2 tsp arrowroot powder
½ tsp vanilla
1 pinch of salt
1 pinch of stevia

Put them all into the blender and blend them thoroughly. Then run the "milk" through a strainer to remove the oat particles. The oat particles can be made into an oatmeal, so you can use all the parts of the recipe.

Non-dairy butter replacement

Ghee is a traditional non-dairy butter replacement made from butter but with all the water and milk solids removed. You can buy ghee from

Indian grocery stores, or you can make your own. Making ghee is incredibly simple.

Put butter into a pot on the stove. Heat it until it boils, stirring occasionally. Once it's reached a boil, lower the temperature. It will froth and foam. When it stops frothing and there is a clear yellow layer on the top and a white layer of sediment on the bottom. Turn the burner back up slightly to make sure that all the boiling is done.

Once you are sure it is done boiling, then you can pour it through a strainer layered with several pieces of fine cheesecloth so the sediment in the bottom of the pan doesn't go through into the golden liquid. This is ghee. There is not an official amount of time that ghee will keep. If you make sure to remove all of the water and milk solids, ghee should keep for a good period of time in a sealed airtight container.

Dairy-free cheese

Making a dairy free cheese replacement is a little more complicated, but definitely doable.

Here's the recipe:

1 cup warm water

2 T gelatin (or agar powder for vegans)

1 T oat fiber

½ T coconut flour

1 tsp flax meal (grind just before use)

¾ tsp collagen

¼ Glucomannan powder

¾ tsp salt

1 tsp onion powder ¼ tsp dry mustard powder 1 T smoked paprika

¼ tsp cayenne pepper

¼ C nutritional yeast

2 T lemon juice (for food storage – you can purchase lemon juice packets)

1 T Integral Collagen

2 tsp toasted sesame oil

2 tsp Tahini

1 tsp liquid smoke

Directions: Heat the water to boiling. Add 2 tablespoons of gelatin and reduce heat. Whisk in oat fiber, coconut flour, flax meal, collagen, and glucomannan. Once incorporated, turn off heat. Add the rest of the ingredients. Once completely incorporated, pour into a bowl, cover with plastic wrap and refrigerate. Once it hardens in the fridge, you'll be able to slice it, shred it, or even melt it.

Egg Free

Egg free diets take a little more discernment on how to replace the eggs, than it being a **straight** one to one. You need to first ask yourself if the eggs called for in the recipe are for leavening or for binding.

An example of when eggs are used as a leavening agent would be in brownies. Many brownie recipes do not call for baking powder or baking soda. The eggs help leaven the brownies. When I make meatloaf, I use eggs in my recipe. I don't use them to help the meatloaf rise, but to bind the meat and oats together to make the loaf. This is an example of using the eggs as a binding agent.

If you need eggs to leaven your recipe there are several possible egg replacements. First is a commercial egg replacement called Ener-G. You should be able to find this at most Asian markets. Another option for eggs as a leavening agent is one teaspoon of ground flax seeds or chia seeds and one quarter of a cup of water. A third option—probably the best for long-term food storage—is one teaspoon of baking soda and one tablespoon of apple cider vinegar.

If you need to use eggs as a binder, you can use whole-wheat flour (if you don't have gluten issues), cornstarch, or mashed potatoes. You would add one tablespoon at a time until the mixture binds together properly.

Vegetarian and Vegan

There is a distinct difference between a vegetarian and vegan diet, but short or long-term food storage concerns would be similar or have already been addressed.

Vegans would need a replacement for eggs, milk, and cheese. These have already been addressed in this chapter. The other problem that vegans could run into with food storage is finding healthy fats. Olive oil is an appropriate solution for short-term food storage if you don't plan on heating it, but if you need to heat the oil, the best option would be coconut oil. Coconut oil keeps for eighteen months to three years and can be heated in high heat.

With dairy products and oils taken care of, the main concern that vegans and vegetarians have in common is getting enough protein in their diets through food storage.

There are several options for this. Most food storage companies will have options to get food with TVP or Textured Vegetable Protein. This is usually a soy-based protein, made to have a similar consistency to whatever protein it is replacing in the recipe. Another option would be to include beans in your food storage—sprouted beans contain even more protein than unsprouted. You should also use your garden. There are various kinds of vegetables that contain protein. Lima beans, green peas, succotash, kale, broccoli, white mushrooms, cooked corn, artichoke, and spinach also score high in protein per cup.

We've taken a good look at several specialty diets and how to overcome the difficulties that they can impose upon us. These diets can be a challenge, but being a challenge isn't the same things as being impossible. We can do this. These substitutions and suggestions should help.

We've covered so much in the book so far, but sometimes, it's easy to get tunnel vision and miss things that will make our lives easier if we have to live on our food storage. In the next chapter, we're going to talk about some of our blind spots and make sure that we take care of them as well.

Chapter Seven Assignment:

1. If you have any food allergies or sensitivities, pick two replacements and try them in different recipes or try the recipe given here in this chapter.

If you aren't sure where to find items mentioned in this chapter or you want my specific recommendations, you can find them listed in the Resource Center of the website: https://www.ayearwithoutthegrocerystore.com/single-post/2017/12/07/Resource-Center

Chapter Eight
Food Storage Blind Spots

When we get focused on the ins and outs of food storage, sometimes there are important aspects that we may miss to our detriment. In this chapter we're going to cover the blind spots that many people have when it comes to food storage and how to plug those holes so that you're better prepared.

Storing Water

Most of the time, when we talk about being prepared or about food storage, we think of dehydrated foods, but we don't think about what we will need to rehydrate those foods—water. Most people have heard the saying: you can last three minutes without air, three days without water, and three weeks without food, but we often focus on the item that we can last three weeks without instead of focusing on the item we can only live three days without.

Water storage should be almost as much, if not more, of a priority for storage than food is. When we talk water storage, there are lots of different ways that it can be accomplished. Some options cost nothing but the water, some cost more for convenience. Having water stored in several different ways is very helpful because water is used for different purposes, so having water in different sized containers makes sense. Water weighs eight pounds per gallon. That means a fifty-five-gallon barrel weighs 440 pounds. It's not easy to move around, but a case of water weighs approximately twenty-four pounds. This is much more easily handled.

The fastest way to store water is in the largest containers. While there are larger containers, fifty-five-gallon barrels are the easiest to obtain, clean, and fill. At one gallon of water per person, per day, one fifty-five-gallon barrel would last a single person almost two months, or a family of four about two weeks.

If you are going to store water in fifty-five-gallon plastic water barrels, there are two ways to go about it. You can buy them brand new from the store, or you can buy them used. The benefit to buying them new is that you know nothing has been stored in them that could contaminate the water. The benefits to buying them used is they cost a fraction of what new barrels cost. No matter which type you decide to purchase, make sure they are made from FDA-approved material. They should be opaque blue in color to discourage the growth of algae or microorganisms.

If you purchase used fifty-five-gallon plastic water barrels, make sure that the food or liquid stored in them were fit for human consumption. Even then, make sure you clean them out extremely well. Once you fill them with water, new and used fifty-five-gallon water barrels both need an eighth of a cup of bleach. The bleach must be 5–6 percent sodium hypochlorite, with no colors or scents and no other active ingredients. Most water from municipal sources is treated with chlorine to kill germs and bacteria. In food storage, I use bleach to the same purpose. Stagnant water can provide a rich place to grow microorganisms, germs, and bacteria. Bleach will kill the germs. Before I drink stored water, I use my Berkey water filter to clean the chlorine and anything else potentially detrimental out of the water.

Other items you will need to go along with the water barrels are a bung wrench, manual siphon pump, and a water filter. Despite your best efforts, something might get into your water. It is always better to have a safety redundancy when it comes to drinking water. I would highly suggest purchasing a Berkey Water filter in order to make sure the water that you use is safe. Berkey is known for its ability to filter, "harmful pathogenic bacteria, cysts, parasites, and unhealthy chemical contaminants such as chlorine to levels higher than 99.99%, while at the same time leaving in the essential minerals your body needs."[8] This water filtration system is gravity fed, so you don't need electricity to use it. It will filter out anything that didn't get cleaned out of any barrel as well as the chlorine that you put in the barrel to deter the growth of pathogens and protozoa.

If you have some notice that an event is going to take place, like a hurricane, another very helpful item is called a WaterBob. This is a liner designed to fit into a standard bathtub. It holds 100 gallons of water. If you have two bathtubs and two WaterBobs, you have 200 gallons of fresh water that could last a family of four up to fifty days at one gallon of water per

---

[8] (www.bigberkeywaterfilters.com)

person per day. The WaterBob is designed to keep water useable up to sixteen weeks.

There are other size containers each right for their own types of jobs. Five-gallon camping water containers are very helpful for washing hands because they have a spigot on them. They are heavy to move around, weighing in at forty pounds, but can easily be refilled by using smaller containers.

Another helpful type of water container is called a WaterBrick. These hold three gallons of water, and weigh twenty-four pounds. It holds a good deal of water, but isn't too heavy to be moved around. WaterBricks are made to stack, so you can get a good amount of water into a compact space. Also, they are made of opaque blue plastic so as to discourage growth of any algae or bacteria.

Empty two-liter soda containers can be used for short-term water storage, especially if they are stored in the freezer until needed. They are a good size to easily move water around and to use to refill the five-gallon camping water containers. They aren't made of blue opaque plastic, so they need to be frozen so as to not let algae grow. If power does go out, they need to be used quickly once they thaw.

Last but not least there are half-liter plastic water bottles. They provide a great way to stay hydrated with each meal. They are portioned out so that you keep your drinking water usage in check while also keeping your thirst in check. They are so light and convenient to carry around and easy to refill from larger containers. You don't want them sitting around long though since they are in clear plastic bottles. If you keep them on hand, you will need to rotate through them.

If you are lucky enough to have a well on your property, you may feel confident in not storing any water. Storing water is still important. If power goes out, you will be without water, unless you have a strong enough hand pump to draw the water from the well to a container. Finding your pump and getting it set up will take time. Having water stored will still be necessary and helpful in any type of emergency situation.

Since water is one of the most precious commodities, but because it is so heavy, it's hard to haul around in large quantities. Sometimes this necessitates a portable way to filter water. There are two great ways to filter water on the run. The Berkey Sport bottle is an efficient way to filter water. You can collect water from a potentially unsafe water source if you need to keep moving. Another portable way to filter water is called a life straw. You drink from a body of water through the straw. You can't carry any water with you using it, but it will filter pathogens out of the water that you find and allow you to drink it safely.

Spices

While water makes it possible for you to live, spices make it palatable while you live. It's one thing to have food to eat, but it's another thing to have to eat bland food every day because no one thought to store spices. Spices are the difference between curry chicken and Italian chicken. The chicken is just chicken, but because there are spices, the difference in taste is night and day.

Salt is the first spice to start with. It's not easily made, which makes it invaluable to store. Salt flavors food and preserves food. It's also incredibly inexpensive and can help you get the iodine you need if you store iodized salt. If you store sea salt instead, it helps provide trace minerals that everyone needs. Salt is the difference between tasteful and bland. You can currently purchase #50 bags of sea salt from Azure Standard for thirty-five dollars. That's one of the best investments you can make.

Each year our church does a chili cook-off. One year, I entered a white chicken chili. Normally I used canned beans in the chili. This time, I decided to soak and cook the beans myself. Even with all the other ingredients being the same, it tasted awful. Unfortunately, I didn't taste it until after I entered. Once I did, I tried to figure out what I did differently. All the ingredients were the same as every other time I had made it except for the canned beans. Canned beans have a good deal of salt in them. I didn't take into account the salt from the canned beans when I soaked the beans myself. Salt made the difference between barely edible and really scrumptious.

Pepper is the second most useful spice. Salt and pepper sit together on tables. Salt gives something flavor, pepper gives something a little kick. If you only had the ability to store two seasonings, salt and pepper would probably be it, but storing more than two seasonings would be highly recommended. Costco, Sam's Club, and Azure Standard are among the best places to purchase black pepper in bulk.

Chili powder is another staple spice. Chili is one of the easiest food storage meals to make, but it won't taste worth eating if there is no chili powder in it. Packets of chili mix cost more than a dollar per packet in most places, but a sixteen-ounce container of chili mix (which should make about eight pots of chili, even if you like it spicy) costs between four and six dollars. Chili powder is also used in so many other great food storage meals like tortilla soup and Mexicale pie. It's also a main component of taco seasoning, which is in other Mexican meals like tacos, enchilada meat, fajitas, and other meals.

Taco Seasoning Recipe

1 C chili powder
½ C onion powder
¼ C cumin
3 T garlic
3 T paprika
2 T salt

Onion powder is a part of so many mixes. It's used in the above taco seasoning recipe. I use it in my Italian dressing recipe, my spaghetti mix recipe, and others. The best places to buy onion powder are Costco, Sam's, or Azure standard. It's really not worth it buying it any other places. It's almost always too expensive for too little spice. It is possible to make it yourself.

Onion powder is made by peeling your onions chopping them into small pieces, and putting them through a food mill. Deluxe Food Strainer and Sauce Maker by VICTORIO VKP250 is my favorite to use. Spread the mixture on parchment paper and put it on the lowest setting in an oven or put the mixture on Paraflexx sheets and put them in your dehydrator. Once it's dry, put it through a blender to powder it.

Italian Dressing Mix

2 T onion powder

1 T garlic powder
1 ½ T parsley
1 T tsp oregano
4 tsp salt
1 ½ tsp pepper
1 tsp celery flakes
1 tsp basil
½ tsp thyme

To make the mix into a dressing for a family take one-quarter of a cup of your dressing mix, and add half a cup of apple cider vinegar, one tablespoon of water, and one cup of olive oil. Mix thoroughly.

For single serving, take two tablespoons of your dressing mix, one-quarter of a cup of apple cider vinegar, two teaspoons of water, and half a cup of olive oil. Mix thoroughly.

Garlic powder is another spice I seem to use in everything. Besides being in my taco seasoning mix and my Italian dressing mix, I also use it in my ranch dressing mix and spaghetti mix. Garlic pairs well with so many other seasonings; it adds a robust flavor to any dish. Garlic is easily grown, and can keep. One of the benefits of garlic powder is that it gives a little less pungent flavor than straight garlic.

Garlic powder can be made in a similar manner to onion powder. After you break off the cloves of garlic and peel them, chop them coarsely put them through a food mill. Spread the resulting mixture onto parchment paper and place them on the lowest setting of your oven or spread it onto Paraflexx sheets and use a dehydrator.

Spaghetti Mix

C flour or arrowroot powder
3 T Basil
2 T Oregano
2 tsp thyme
2 tsp garlic powder
1 tsp parsley
½ tsp onion powder

1 tsp salt
1 tsp pepper

On medium heat, blend the mix with some fat in a pan (either added to the pan or left over from browning meat). Slowly add tomato sauce to the mix on the stove.

Oregano, Basil, Parsley, and Thyme

All of these herbs are used heavily in Italian dishes. They are so easy to grow, but if you don't want to grow them, buy them in bulk. Italian dishes are one of the easiest ways to grow your food storage, so growing or storing oregano and basil makes good sense.

If you decide to grow these plants and you want to have the spices available over the winter, you can bring them inside in a pot or you can dehydrate the stalks and leaves. Once you've dried the leaves, they pull away from the stalks easily. Rub the leaves between your hands to break them up and keep them in a sealed canning jar through the cold months of the year. The other option is to buy them from the same places that have been mentioned to acquire the rest of your spices.

Ranch Dressing Mix

C onion powder
2 T parsley flakes
4 tsp salt
1 tsp garlic powder

Mix these together and store them in an airtight container. To make Ranch Dressing, mix two tablespoons of the dry mix with one cup of mayonnaise (you can make from scratch) and one cup of buttermilk (which you will find in Chapter 9's food storage recipes).

All the spices we've mentioned so far have been savory, but there are plenty of sweet spices too that you'll want to have on hand, such as cinnamon. We use cinnamon in everything from muffins to making our own ketchup. It's not something easily grown, so it's an ideal candidate for food storage.

Ketchup

6 oz can tomato paste
¾ C water
2 T Apple Cider Vinegar
2 T honey or sugar
1 tsp salt
½ tsp onion powder
¼ tsp cinnamon
¼ tsp cloves
1/8 tsp cayenne

Many times most other sweet spices go together: cloves, ginger, nutmeg and allspice. Ginger can be grown fairly easily, but cloves, nutmeg, and allspice are not easily grown in the United States. The best course of action is to store them. You can mix up the cinnamon, ginger, nutmeg, and cloves together and keep it for use in other sweet items such as yogurt, applesauce, and other baked fruits.

Sweet Seasoning Mix

¼ C cinnamon
1 T ginger
1 T nutmeg
1 T cloves

Mix together and store in a jar.

The following recipe is one of our favorite recipes that calls for spices that are usually associated with sweet foods.

Honey Pecan Apple Crisp (serves eight)

8 C chopped apples
1 T Sweet Seasoning Mix
¼ tsp salt
¼ C honey
⅓ C Coconut oil
1 ½ C pecans

1. Peel, core, and slice the apples.
2. Sprinkle 2 tsp of the spices over the apples.
3. Finely chop the pecans. Mix pecans, honey, coconut oil, and one teaspoon of seasonings.
4. Top the apples with this mixture. Bake at 375 degrees for thirty-five to forty minutes.

Extracts

Extracts are easily made whether they are vanilla, peppermint, or lemon. Each can be made by steeping the item in vodka. Vodka will keep indefinitely. While the amount of flavor may vary with the length of time that you store your extracts, they won't go bad if you make them yourself.

Making vanilla extract is as simple as cutting twenty vanilla beans into one-inch pieces in, and putting them in a one-quart jar. Fill the quart jar with vodka. Put a lid on the jar and store it in a cool dark place for three months. Shake the jar occasionally. After three months, strain the liquid off and discard the vanilla beans. The extract is best stored in a dark colored glass bottle.

Peppermint extract is made the same way. Cut some peppermint from a plant. Pulling the leaves off the plant will give you more flavor than putting whole stems in. Pack one to two cups of peppermint leaves into a quart jar. Fill the quart jar with vodka and shake. Put in a cool dark place for three months. Shake the jar occasionally. After three months, strain the liquid off and discard the peppermint leaves. The extract is best stored in a dark colored glass bottle.

Lemon extract is an extract made from the flavor of lemon rinds. To make lemon extract you peel the lemon and cut the rinds into strips, then into pieces. Use about two cups of lemon rind to one quart of vodka. Fill the quart jar with vodka and shake. Put in a cool dark place for three months. Shake the jar occasionally. After three months, strain the liquid off and discard the lemon rinds. The extract is best stored in a dark colored glass bottle.

Baking Supplies

Most people remember to store flour, sugar, and brown sugar, but there are other baking supplies that are easily overlooked including baking powder, baking soda, cream of tartar, arrowroot powder or cornstarch, and yeast.

Baking powder is a leavening agent for many homemade baked goods. Baking powder is expensive, however, and what do you do when you run out? Even though it's expensive, it is easily made by taking a 1:1:2 ratio of baking soda, arrowroot powder, and cream of tartar. You can make this by the teaspoon or by the cup, it doesn't matter. For explanation purposes, we'll use a cup. To make this you would take one cup of baking soda, one cup of arrowroot powder, and two cups of cream of tartar. Azure Standard has these items at better prices than anywhere else, even Costco and Sam's Club. You likely won't find cream of tartar at Costco or Sam's anyway.

Besides using arrowroot powder in baking powder, it is a wonderful thickener. To use arrowroot powder as a thickener, remove some of the hot liquid from whatever it is you want to thicken, add one to two tablespoons of arrowroot powder and mix it thoroughly so that it's not clumpy, but thick. Pour that liquid back into what it is you want to thicken, and it will thicken it very well.

Yeast is another baking supply that you will need for your food storage, whether short-term or long-term. Yeast keeps longer if you buy it in vacuum-sealed packages. For purposes of food storage, you should purchase your yeast in #1 vacuum-sealed packs. If you make bread with any regularity, the small pouches of yeast will not last very long, and besides, they will cost a whole lot more money. Sam's and Costco are great places to get your yeast.

Vitamins, Supplements, and Digestive First Aid

Stress takes its toll on anyone's body. Throw your body into a situation which is not only unfamiliar, but more stressful than usual and potentially frightening, and your immune system takes a huge hit. Add not getting the level of nutrition that your body is used to, more than likely getting less sleep than you are accustomed, and it's a perfect storm for sickness when life is already hard.

One way to help bolster your body during a stressful or difficult situation is through vitamins and supplements. Having a good stock of vitamins and supplements on hand for such an occasion is going to help your body make the transition from normal to stressful more easily. Keep in mind vitamins and supplements do have expiration dates, so you will want to rotate through them.

Besides picking up a multi-vitamin, consider purchasing something along the lines of the Emergen-C dietary supplement. It is designed specifically to help your immune system remain healthy.

You know your family well enough to know how your digestive tracts handle unusual foods and stressful situations. Having items on hand for specifically dealing with stomach issues before an emergency of any type strikes is very helpful.

Activated charcoal is potentially a lifesaving item to have on hand. Hospitals used to give activated charcoal to people who ingested poisons or had an accidental overdose. Activated charcoal has many other applications as well. You can find it in drug stores. It is marketed to help upset stomachs and digestive issues.

To keep our stomach's functioning optimally, we also keep essential oils on hand. Peppermint is a very helpful essential oil to keep stomachs feeling their best. I will often use a Young Living supplement called NingXia Red along with a couple of drops of peppermint. DiGize, an essential blend made by Young Living, is another essential oil blend which helps maintain the health of the rest of the digestive tract below the stomach.

Does your family use antacids, Pepto-Bismol, or another similar product? Make sure that you have things on hand that your family uses, whether it's "The pink stuff" or crackers and ginger ale. Be prepared to help your family feel better.

Make sure that as you gather items to help your family whether it's through a financial struggle, a power outage, or a natural disaster. Look for areas that you may have holes in your food storage and related items and take steps to plug those holes. Plugging the holes in our food storage helps us use especially our long-term food storage effectively. In our next chapter I'm going to take it to another level and teach you how to use more parts of your long-term food storage effectively.

Chapter Eight Assignments

1. Choose three recipes from the chapter, and try them
2. On a scale of 1–10, 1 being "I have none" and 10 being "I have an indefinite supply of water," rate your water supply. What steps are you going to take to increase your supply of water?
3. List three spices that you have an adequate supply stored for a year. List three spices that you need to pick up a years supply. List three spices that you will start growing yourself.
4. Do you have a three-month supply of vitamins for everyone in your family? If not, add vitamins to your next grocery trip.
5. List any other items from this chapter that you need to make sure to stock up on in the next month.

If you aren't sure where to find items mentioned in this chapter or you want my specific recommendations, you can find them listed in the Resource Center of the website:

https://www.ayearwithoutthegrocerystore.com/single-post/2017/12/07/Resource-Center

Chapter Nine
Making the Most of the Basics

When you get started with long-term food storage, it's easy to look at buckets and think, "What am I going to make out of *this*?" Learning to make things from the basics can make all the difference in the world.

This chapter is about making sense out of your basic ingredients in those buckets, what essentials can be made from these ingredients, and what other recipes these essentials can be used in.

Oftentimes people collect buckets with powdered milk, wheat berries, dried corn, dried beans, rice, rolled oats, and sugar. Let's learn how to use them.

Powdered Milk

Powdered milk makes a whole lot more than milk. You can get really creative with it and make evaporated milk, sweetened condensed milk, "Magic Mix" milk, and more. You can make amazing things from just having powdered milk.

Milk

This is, of course, what everyone expects to make with powdered milk. It can be made with

¼ C + 1 T dry milk mix

1 C water

If you want it a little sweeter, add half a teaspoon of sugar and a splash of vanilla.

How to you make evaporated milk from powdered milk?

Evaporated Milk

1 C powdered milk

1 ½ C water

Evaporated Milk can be used in so many kinds of recipes including biscuits and gravy, macaroni and cheese, chocolate fudge sauce, and pasta alfredo.

Sawmill gravy—This recipe contains the above recipe for evaporated milk doubled

2 T butter or ghee

¼ C flour3C water

2C powdered milk1 tsp salt

½ tsp pepper

Directions:
1. In a saucepan, heat the water and add the 2C powdered milk
2. Melt two tablespoons of butter in a pan on the stove. Mix in the flour
3. Slowly whisk the into the butter and /flour mixture.
4. Add spices and continue to whisk as it thickens.

Cheese Sauce (can be used with cooked pasta for macaroni and cheese)

1 recipe evaporated milk

1 C rehydrated cheese

1 T arrowroot powder

2 tsp hot sauce or ¼ tsp cayenne pepper

Directions:
1. Rehydrate cheese of your choice. Mix with arrowroot powder.
2. Heat evaporated milk recipe on the stove. Add hot sauce or cayenne pepper. Whisk the cheese and arrowroot powder in a little at a time.
3. Continue to whisk and let thicken as it heats.

Beef Stroganoff

2 C Beef Crumbles

2 ¼ C water

1 recipe evaporated milk

3 cans sliced mushrooms drained

#1 uncooked egg noodles

1 C prepared sour cream (from sour cream powder)

¼ apple cider vinegar

3 T dry milk powder

1 tsp liquid smoke

2 T chives

Directions:

1. Prepare your egg noodles according to package directions.
2. In a large pan, whisk the recipe for evaporated milk, prepared sour cream powder, water, dry milk powder, apple cider vinegar, and liquid smoke together over medium heat.
3. Once incorporated, reduce heat to low and add beef crumbles.
4. Continue to cook on the stove, slowly stirring until thickened.

Sweetened Condensed Milk

Sweetened Condensed milk has so many uses, and it's so simple to make.

½ C hot water

1 C dry powdered milk

¾ C sugar

2 T ghee

½ tsp vanilla

Fudge, Carmel, and other delicious desserts

Fudge

1 recipe sweetened condensed milk

1 -12 oz bag chocolate chips

2 T ghee

1 tsp vanilla

1. Heat sweetened condensed milk, chocolate chips, and ghee over a medium low heat
2. Once combined add vanilla and stir.
3. Pour into a lined eight- by eight-inch pan and chill.

Carmel

Ingredients:

1 recipe sweetened condensed milk

1. Put the "sweetened condensed milk" into a canning jar with a regular canning lid and ring. Tighten the ring so no water gets into the jar.
2. Submerse the jar completely in a large pot. Make sure the jar stays covered with water at all times.
3. Simmer on low for about three hours. Using canning tongs, remove the jar. You should have caramel.

Rice Pudding

What a great way to use three of the ingredients or recipes from our food storage!

1 ½ C water
1 recipe sweetened condensed milk
1 recipe evaporated milk
½ C rice
½ C raisins
½ tsp cinnamon
Pinch salt

Directions:

1. Heat the water on the stove, add the rice and a pinch of salt.
2. Cover and simmer about twenty minutes.
3. Stir in evaporated milk and sweetened condensed milk until rice is tender.
4. Turn off the heat, stir in raisins and cinnamon and serve.

Sweetened condensed milk can also be used in salted caramels, pound cake, chocolate frosting, key lime pie, chocolate truffles, and more.

"Magic Mix"

Magic Mix is an amazing mix that you can make up ahead of time and keep in the fridge if you have power. If you don't have power, this should still keep at room temperature. From it you can make so many different things, both sweet and savory! It truly is "Magic!"

2 ¼ C instant nonfat dry milk
1 C ghee
1 C flour

Alfredo sauce

1 C water
½ C Magic Mix
¼ C parmesan cheese
1 tsp garlic powder
½ tsp onion powder

Directions: Whisk ingredients over medium heat on the stove until thick.

Gravy

1 C Magic Mix
2 C chicken or beef broth

Directions: Whisk ingredients over medium heat on the stove until it reaches serving temperature.

Cream of Chicken Soup

1 C Magic Mix
¾ C chicken broth
½ tsp onion powder
½ tsp garlic powder
1 tsp nutritional yeast (optional)

Directions: Whisk ingredients over medium heat on the stove until it reaches serving temperature.

Cream of Mushroom Soup

1 C Magic Mix
2 cans mushroom pieces
½ tsp onion powder

½ garlic powder
½ tsp nutritional yeast

Directions:

1. Drain liquid from mushroom pieces and reserve.
2. Add enough water to the liquid from the mushroom pieces to make three-quarters of a cup of liquid
3. Whisk liquid, Magic Mix, and spices on medium heat on the stove.

Condensed Tomato Soup

1 C Magic Mix
1 ½ C water
½ C tomato powder
½ tsp salt
¼ tsp pepper

Directions: Whisk ingredients over medium heat on the stove until it reaches serving temperature.

Vanilla Pudding

1 C Magic Mix
½ C sugar
2 C water
2 tsp vanilla

Directions:

1. Mix Magic Mix and sugar in a saucepan
2. Slowly whisk in water. Bring to a simmer until it begins to thicken.
3. Remove from heat and briskly whisk in vanilla. Let cool and serve.

To make chocolate pudding add three tablespoons of chocolate and one-quarter of a teaspoon of salt to the Magic Mix and sugar in the sauce pan. Reduce the vanilla to one teaspoon.

Oats

The oats in your food storage buckets can be used in different ways. Most of us would say, well, of course, we can use the oats for oatmeal. That's a given.

Crumbles

Using oats in a crumble recipe is a great way to eat them other than as oatmeal. You can use apples, strawberries, blueberries, blackberries, raspberries, pears, peaches, or other fruit in "crumble" recipes. A crumble recipe is where you take fruit and either mash it or slice it up, sprinkle it with just a smidge of sweetener and cover it with a topping. The topping is partially made of oats.

Crumble Recipes (serves 4)

4 cups fruit
⅓ C sweetener (sugar or honey)
2 C oats
½ C ghee
½ brown sugar or honey
1 tsp cinnamon, cloves, or nutmeg
1 tsp vanilla

Directions:
1. Preheat oven to 375 degrees.
2. Combine either sliced or whole fruit with the sweetener and mix thoroughly. Pour into a greased eight- by eight-inch pan.
3. In a separate bowl, mix oats, brown sugar or honey, spices, and vanilla.
4. Cut the mixture into the ghee. Sprinkle mixture over top of the fruit.
5. Bake at 375 degrees for thirty minutes.

Granola

Another familiar way to use oats is granola. It also uses plenty of other things that can be stored in your long-term food storage. The recipe below is just one example. You can use any ingredients that you have on hand after baking, including dried dates, apricots, plums, pumpkin seeds, or freeze-dried fruit. It is a hearty snack or cereal.

Granola Recipe

6 C oats

1 C raisins

1 C sunflower seeds

1 C shredded coconut

1 C nuts (any kind you have on hand)

⅔ C coconut oil

⅔ C honey

1 tsp vanilla

Directions:

1. Mix the oats, raisins, sunflower seeds, coconut, and nuts in a glass baking dish.
2. Melt the coconut oil and honey in a saucepan on top of the stove. Add the teaspoon of vanilla.
3. Pour the liquid mixture over the dry ingredient mixture and stir thoroughly.
4. Bake it at 250 degrees in your conventional oven or HERC oven for one hour.

You'll find a recipe for milk that you can make on your own from oats in the chapter on Specialty Diets

Granola Bars

A specialized use of granola is granola bars.

2 C oats

1 C natural peanut butter

½ C peanuts

½ C raisins or dates

¼ C honey

½ tsp salt

Directions: Mix all ingredients. Line an eight- by eight-inch pan with parchment paper. Press the mixture into the lined pan. Let harden. Refrigerator works best, but counter will do.

Oats in Baking

Blueberry Bread

½ C freeze-dried blueberries, rehydrated

1 ¾ C flour or gluten free flour mix

½ C old fashion oats

1 ½ tsp baking powder

½ tsp baking soda

½ tsp salt

½ tsp cinnamon

¼ tsp cloves

1 cup sugar

4 T egg powder

⅓ C water

1 tsp vanilla

¼ C + 1T dry milk powder

1 C water

1 T vinegar

⅓ C water

Directions:
1. Preheat the oven, HERC oven, or solar oven to 350 degrees
2. Toss the rehydrated berries with one tablespoon of flour.
3. Mix flour, oats, baking powder, baking soda, salt, cinnamon, and nutmeg. Set aside.
4. Mix sugar, egg powder, one-third of a cup of water, and vanilla together.
5. In a separate cup, mix dry milk powder, one cup of water, and vinegar. Let sit for five minutes.
6. Add to sugar, egg powder, water, and vanilla.
7. Add the liquid mixture to the dry mixture stirring gently.
8. Bake in a greased loaf pan for fifty to sixty minutes.

Ground Oats

Oats can be ground into oat flour, and oat flour can be used for cooking and baking. Pancakes can easily be made with oat flour.

Oat Pancake recipe

1 ½ C oats
¼ tsp salt
½ tsp baking powder
½ tsp cinnamon
2 T egg powder equivalent
¼ C + 1 T dry milk powder
1 ¼ C water
½ tsp vanilla

Directions:

1. Put the oats through either a blender or food processor.
2. Mix the oats and the rest of the ingredients in a large bowl.
3. Spoon ¼ C of the liquid onto a hot griddle. Cook on the first side until it bubbles. Flip and heat until thoroughly cooked.

Oat Pie Crust

3 C oats (ground in a blender)
1 tsp salt
½ C flour (or gluten free flour equivalent)
½ C ghee
1 C sugar
1 T molasses
3 T melted ghee

Directions:

1. Combine oats, salt, and flour in a blender. Blend well.
2. Cream half of a cup of ghee, sugar, and molasses together.
3. Add dry ingredients until well incorporated. Spread the mixture over a lined cookie sheet.
4. Bake for ten minutes at 350 degrees.

5. Crumble the mixture and stir it around mixing it well. Spread it out again and bake for another ten minutes.

6. Pull it out of the oven and break it into pieces again. Put it back into your blender and powder it as best as possible. Remove it.

7. Slowly pour the melted ghee in one tablespoon at a time and mix thoroughly. Once incorporated, press into a pie plate and chill.

Wheat

When we say "wheat" most people translate that word in their heads to "flour." And while flour comes from wheat, there is so much more you can do with wheat than make flour for baked goods.

That being said, wheat is easily ground into flour using a grain grinder. There are both electric and non-electric versions.

My favorite bread recipe comes from Paula's Bread.

Here's her recipe:

Paula's Whole Wheat Bread (5 Loaves)—Used with permission (https://www.paulasbread.com/recipes.html#5loaves)

5 ½ cup warm water (about 100 to 105 degrees)

3 T SAF instant yeast

1 T Dough Enhancer

⅔ cup oil

⅔ honey

2 T salt

15-18 cups whole-wheat flour

1. Place all ingredients in your Bosch Universal Mixer with seven cups of whole-wheat flour. Turn Bosch Stand Mixer on Speed 1.

2. Slowly add the remaining whole-wheat flour until the dough pulls away from the sides of the bowl, about eight more cups. Mix or knead for four minutes.

3. Form into five whole-wheat loaves and place in Stainless Steel bread pans to rise once. Bake at 350 degrees for twenty to twenty-five minutes. Enjoy!

Meat Supplement or Substitute

If you get to the point where you want to start conserving the meat that you have in your house, you have two options. You can either cut the amount of meat you use in certain recipes (like chili or tacos) or you can add something to the meat to supplement or stretch it.

Believe it or not, wheat can be used to stretch your meat. It's as simple as using one cup of wheat berries. Pulse them through your blender or through a coffee grinder (there are non-electric forms of each). Once you've cracked the wheat, add it to two cups of water and bring to a boil. Boil for twelve to fifteen minutes or until it's tender. You'll want to spice it up, but this one cup of wheat will replace one pound of ground beef.

If you've never attempted it before, you can cook up one cup of wheat berries like described and add it to a pound of ground beef for tacos. See what your family thinks before going completely without meat.

Cream of Wheat

Cream of wheat goes through much of the same process.

2 C cracked wheat (wheat put through pulse on a blender or coffee grinder)

1 C water

1 ¼ C powdered milk

1 tsp vanilla

¼ C honey or maple syrup

Directions:

1. Heat the water, powdered milk and vanilla on the stove.
2. Whisk in two cups of cracked wheat until it thickens. Once thickened, add the sweetener.

Cooked Wheat Berries

Wheat berries can be cooked up simply and eaten like oatmeal or added to other recipes.

Serves 2

1 C Wheat Berries

2 C Boiling Water

½ tsp salt

Sweetener of your choice

Directions:

1. Add boiling water, wheat berries, and salt to a thermos.
2. Let sit eight to twelve hours.
3. Remove and drain excess liquid. Add sweetener of your choice and serve.
4. You can also add this recipe to yogurt, to salads (in place of sunflower seeds), alongside your ground beef (bulgur wheat works better).

Sprouted Wheat

Sprouting wheat berries multiplies nutrients and neutralizes natural inhibitors that block the absorption of iron, copper, magnesium, and calcium. Sprouting wheat berries also increases the enzymes that can be found in the berries. Once sprouted, they can be dehydrated and ground into flour to use.

Directions:

1. Take one cup of wheat berries, rinse them and pull out any debris. Place wheat berries in a half-gallon sized jar. Fill the jar with water and cover with a mesh screen. Soak at least six hours or overnight.
2. Drain the wheat berries. Turn the jar upside down in a bowl so the berries will continue to drain while also allowing air to flow around the berries.
3. After twelve hours, rinse and drain again. Do this for two to three days.
4. You'll start to notice tails emerging from the wheat. When you do, the wheat is sprouted.

At this point you can dehydrate the sprouted wheat. You need to use a dehydrator because you can't dry the wheat berries at any temperature above 113 degrees or you will destroy the enzymes, one of the reasons that you want to sprout your wheat berries in the first place.

Wheat Grass

If you take your wheat berries and sprout them, you can grow wheat grass. You can take the wheat grass, cut it, dehydrate it, and powder it. That powder can be an incredible boost to your family's health during tough times.

1. First, gather your wheat berries, a growing tray with lid from a garden supply store, organic soil enriched with fertilizer or compost. Sprout the berries using the instructions above. Once you see the tails and they are sprouted, add one inch of soil to the growing tray. Water lightly just to moisten soil.
2. Sprinkle sprouted seeds across the soil. Sprinkle soil over the sprouted seeds. Put the cover on the tray. Place in an area of indirect light and a temperature of sixty to eighty degrees.
3. Mist with water daily, and when grass is one to two inches tall, remove the cover. You can harvest at any point after four inches of growth.
4. Take the harvested wheat grass and put it in your regular oven, dehydrator, or HERC Oven. Heat at 150 degrees for about an hour until dry and brittle. Grind in a coffee grinder.

You can add wheat grass to just about anything, but it's better if you add it to room temperature items so as not to destroy the good enzymes that detoxify the liver, give you vitamin C, improve your digestion, reduce inflammation, and so much more.

Beans

Beans are an integral part of food storage, but unlike most other things, beans only have one main use. Yes, you can grind them into flour and use them as thickeners, but the main things you are going to use beans for is a dried staple that contains both carbohydrates and proteins.

While it's not necessary for you to soak beans before you cook them, it's best to soak them. Soaking beans makes cooking the beans much quicker. It also neutralizes the nutrient inhibitors that the beans naturally carry.

Soaking beans is as easy as putting one to two inches of beans on the bottom of a pot, and covering them with three to four inches of water and two tablespoons of vinegar. I prefer apple cider vinegar. Heat the beans and water to about 140 degrees, turn the burner off and soak them for twelve to twenty-four hours.

Tomato Powder

While I usually don't lump tomato powder into long-term food storage since I don't store it in buckets, just like most of the other ingredients in this chapter, there is *so much* you can do with it. Tomato powder is made from dehydrating sliced tomatoes and then powdering them in a blender. You can also buy tomato powder from food storage companies like Thrive Life.

Tomato powder can be made into basics ingredients such as tomato puree, tomato paste, and tomato juice. These can, in turn, be made into so many more things.

Tomato paste is a 1:1 ratio of tomato powder and water.

Tomato puree is a 1:4 ratio of tomato powder to water.

Spaghetti Sauce

4 C water
1 C tomato powder
¼ flour
2 T basil
1 ½ T oregano
1 ½ T parsley
½ T salt
½ T Garlic Powder
½ T onion powder
1 tsp thyme
1 tsp pepper

Mix ingredients together and heat over medium heat.

Ketchup—Here is another variation on a recipe for ketchup

½ C tomato powder

1 ¼ C water

2 T Apple Cider Vinegar

2 T honey

1 tsp salt

½ tsp onion powder

¼ tsp cinnamon

¼ tsp cloves

1/8 tsp cayenne

Mix in a bowl and use immediately or refrigerate.

Barbeque Sauce

1 ketchup recipe above

2 T honey or sugar

½ tsp garlic powder

½ tsp mustard

1 tsp liquid smoke

Mix together and use immediately or refrigerate.

Pizza Sauce

¼ C tomato powder

1 C water

1 T olive oil

½ tsp garlic powder

1 tsp oregano

1 tsp basil

½ tsp salt

¼ tsp pepper

Mix together and put on pizza crust.

Corn

Corn is another staple part of your food storage. There isn't as much to do with corn as many of the other items in your food storage, but it still plays a vital role. Corn can be one of those fun items. You can pop it into popcorn and top it with melted ghee. You can also grind it into cornmeal. Cornmeal can be made into three main items—grits, cornbread, and corn tortillas.

Grits

2 C boiling water
1 C cornmeal
½ tsp salt

Directions:

1. Boil water. Sprinkle one cup of cornmeal into the water and stir or whisk as you go. Once heated through, you can either sweeten it or add cheese, salt and bacon. My family prefers sweet.

Cornbread

2 ½ C flour
1 ¼ C cornmeal
¾ T salt
⅓ C honey
6 T powdered milk
5 T baking powder
⅓ C coconut oil
¼ C powdered eggs
1 ⅔ C water

Directions:

1. Mix ingredients together. Bake in a nine- by thirteen-inch pan at 425 for twenty-five minutes.

Sugar

The last of the main ingredients that we keep in our long-term food storage that I will be covering in this chapter is sugar. Even sugar has its uses other than just as a sweetener.

One of the easiest and most staple recipes in food storage is oftentimes pancakes, but what are pancakes without syrup?

Maple syrup

2 C Sugar

1 C water

2 T molasses

½ tsp maple flavoring

Directions:

1. Bring water to a boil. Add the sugar, molasses, and maple flavor. Heat until the sugar is completely incorporated. Remove from heat and allow to cool.

Lemon syrup

1 C sugar

1 C water

½ C lemon juice

Directions:

1. Bring water to a boil. Add one cup of sugar. Once the sugar is incorporated, take it off the heat and let cool to room temperature. Add one and one-half cups fresh lemon juice.

Chapter Nine Assignments:

1. Choose three things that you haven't made from food storage before to try.
2. Acquire one new food storage tool to assist you with one of these recipes.

Chapter Ten

As the book draws to a close I want to remind you of the first chapter. Never once in my wildest dreams did I ever consider that we would be displaced from our house for what felt like months on end because of a tornado. No one ever thinks anything like that will happen to them. But it did happen to us.

Learn from our family. Learn that being prepared isn't about being scared, but knowing how to react and being prepared to react accordingly if something ever does happen to you. Preparedness and food storage are really about peace of mind. If something happened to my husband and we lost all our income, I would have a year's worth of food to feed my family, but that doesn't mean that I anticipate losing him. It's not about worry, it's about confidence and peace knowing that my family will be taken care of.

Living by this concept has so many benefits. I make one or two two-week menus and stick to them throughout the year. There's no incessant menu planning. There are no really involved meals—unless you want them to be involved. You save time because you don't run to the grocery store weekly, let alone multiple times a week. Because you're working through the same menus, you can double the recipes and freeze them for the following week. You don't waste your ingredients because you know you are working through the food that you have in your house. You don't need to eat out regularly because you know that there is food is in your house, that it's healthy, that your nutritional bases are covered.

Better that you know that your family is cared for in case of an emergency, whether it's a short-term emergency like a power outage or a long-term emergency like a job loss or lay off. You learn to live by frugal principles that will blend into other aspects of your life helping you save money in so many other areas.

All of these things give you another amazing advantage over most people. You can live with peace of mind. You know your family will be taken care of no matter what. You can rest easy at night knowing that you have food for tomorrow and the day after that and the month after that.

When you started this book, maybe you didn't really have an idea of what you were getting yourself into, but with this book you've opened a door. You've opened a door into a self-sustaining lifestyle, into a preparedness lifestyle.

There are so many more aspects of preparedness out there to explore like learning how to implement water catchment systems, learning how to forage, or learning to do laundry without electricity. What about learning to heat and cool your house without electricity and gas? Learning how to take care of animals. Tending to hygiene needs. Self protection and so many other things.

Practice food storage for awhile. Take some time to gather your food and equipment and use them on a regular basis. Once you feel comfortable with that, then take a foray into another aspect of preparedness. Learn it, practice it, and help bring others along the way because knowledge isn't just knowing something, it's living it.

Throughout this book, I have given you Action Steps to take to move your family toward preparedness. Please take time and actually do these steps. Practice using your food storage. If you learn these things now when you don't need them, if you have to do them later when your life, or your joy, or your cleanliness depends on them, you'll be thankful that you learned and practiced these things ahead of time.

When you picked up this book on food storage, you may have thought that going a year without the grocery store was either just a dream or that it was totally unattainable. I hope that as you worked your way through this book you found that the steps by which you can accumulate a year's worth of food storage are doable when you tackle one step at a time and practice as you go along.

So, as this book comes to a close, I want to invite you to store a year's worth of the smiles of your children, sighs of comfort from your husband, peaceful and sleep-filled nights, peace of mind, and tummies filled with healthy nutritional foods in your house, whether it be in your basement or under beds or in closets. It will make your world much happier, peaceful, and healthier.

Photo credit: Paul Downey

Thank you for downloading my book! I feel honored that you'd take the time to buy and read it. I really appreciate all your feedback, and I love hearing my readers' thoughts on my book.

I want your comments to make the next version better!

Please leave us a helpful *REVIEW* on Amazon.
Thanks so much!!

—Karen

About the Author

On Good Friday in 2011, our house in Ferguson, Missouri was hit by an F4 tornado.

Many people write about food storage from their accumulating of food storage during easy times. They have a knowledge of it, but haven't had to really live it.

I haven't written about food storage because of our abundance, but because we've had to live from our food storage out of necessity. We lived through that F4 tornado that hit our house. While the tornado didn't completely destroy our home, we were displaced by it. Having food storage in our house allowed me to literally pack up three weeks' worth of food and take it to the hotel in which the insurance company was putting us up. I didn't have to think about food or menus or about money to eat out every meal. This knowledge gave me the freedom to focus on getting things settled with the insurance company. I had the freedom to keep my kids going and to deal with them not feeling safe. I had the freedom to run to different places to sign documents or make the different phone calls to deal with the devastation the storm wreaked on our home.

Since that time, I've lived through two other life-changing events. I was an eye-witness to the Ferguson riots. No matter which side of the equation you come down on, it was life-changing and eye opening. I also lived through an armed standoff with a knife-wielding man during my family's time at a local homeschool chess club. This taught me the importance of knowing how to react before something happens, so you get it right. You don't have time to think things over. Each of these things taught me a new level of self-sufficiency and preparedness.

I never knew what life was going to throw at me, but my journey to self-sufficiency started with food storage and grew beyond my wildest imaginings.

If you are interested in finding out more about me, Karen Morris, or *A Year Without the Grocery Store*, you can head here: http://ayearwithoutthegrocerystore.com.

If you want to learn more about how you can write a book like I did from start to finish in 3 months, I have a place you can go to get more information.

You don't already have to have a book idea. You don't have to be a great writer. You don't have to be a grammar whiz. You don't even have to love writing.

All you have to have is a passion and a desire to help others. The rest will fall into place.

You can get more information on the process here: https://xe172.isrefer.com/go/sps4fta-vts/bookbrosinc4321

CPSIA information can be obtained
at www.ICGtesting.com
Printed in the USA
BVHW040948170420
577808BV00010B/1533